W9-BWK-420

REVISED EDITION

Mommy-CEO

(Constantly Evaluating Others)

5 GOLDEN RULES

by Jodie Lynn

MOMMY–CEO
(Constantly Evaluating Others) 5 Golden Rules
Revised Edition
by Jodie Lynn

Illustrations by Joyce Abramson

Cover Illustration: Erin Stark, TLC Graphics
Cover Design by TLC Graphics, www.TLCGraphics.com

Note: This book is not intended to replace professional medical
advice. The author and publisher disclaim any responsibility
for any liability, loss or risk, personal or otherwise, which is
incurred as a consequence, directly or indirectly, of the use
and application of any of the contents of this book.
See www.parenttoparent.com for details on more parenting tips.

Copyright © 2001 by Jodie Lynn

All rights reserved. No part of this book may be reproduced in
any form or by any means without the prior written consent of
both the copyright owner and the publisher except in brief
quotes used in reviews.

Library of Congress Catalog card Number: 2001116103

ISBN 0-9659125-4-X

Martin-Ola Press

Martin-Ola Press / Academy Books
10 Cleveland Avenue
Rutland, VT   05701-0757

Printed in The United States

Books can be bought at discount costs for schools or parenting
groups. Contact Jodie Lynn at www.parenttoparent.com for
details or, write to 16572 Manchester Rd. Suite 131, St. Louis,
MO 63040 for regular mail.

DEDICATION

This book is dedicated to my family
for supporting and encouraging me.
And to my mother, who saw the first copy
while looking down from heaven.
You are always in my heart.

Thanks to all the people who inspired me
to write this book. A special thanks to the
parents, doctors, teachers, grandparents
and caregivers who shared their tips.
And to my book designers, Tamara Dever
and Erin Stark (who worked on the inside
and outside design) and to my editor,
Jill Andersen. You are all amazing women
and are talented beyond words.

NOTE

This book is a revised edition. You are given
Five Golden Rules to guide you through
pull-your-hair-out parenting challenges and
many of life's little problems. Use the index.
The tips cover hot topics on "everyday"
parenting dilemmas from pregnancy through
the teenage years with a little humor thrown
in for good taste. Some names have been
changed to protect privacy.

See www.parenttoparent.com for more tips.

CONTENTS

CONTENTS, CONTINUED

INTRODUCTION

Just Like Me

There will be many times within your parenting career when you will wish you had instructions on various parenting skills. Some kind of a manual or plan would be handy. It might possibly prevent problems, or at least help you get through some of the sticky situations a little easier. Consider this book your personal Preventive Maintenance Plan and manual for you and your kids. Like anything else that requires time and upkeep, so do children. If you are a parent or caregiver, then probably like me you are "constantly evaluating others." We all do it. As parents, it's our job to check out all options pertaining to our children. We ask questions about people, places and things that will be associated with our children and/or family team. (A family team is usually made up of members in your immediate family and consists of two or more people.) By constantly evaluating others, we are gathering information to help guide our children/family in making the right choices to keep them in "good running order." The primary goal in raising children to become well-rounded, intelligent individuals will be one of the most challenging careers you'll ever undertake. Whether you work at home, outside the home or have a home office, ALL MOMS ARE WORKING MOMS! With this in mind, your goal as a parent should include guiding your children with a wide range of acceptable levels of cooperation, self-esteem, responsibility, independence, ethics and morals. This can be accomplished easier by becoming a better-tuned-in parent.

If you become a better-tuned-in parent and motivate cooperation from the members of your family team, the chance for family success will be much greater. In this book I hope you will find humor and wisdom to help establish successful parenting as well as a fulfilling life. My five golden rules for family success are to be used as guidelines. There are valuable tips from parents throughout the entire book and many have come right out of my nationally syndicated newspaper column, Parent to Parent. It has a potential readership of 29.7 MILLION readers! Individuals write to me every day. I consider the parents the REAL experts. Please remember each guideline, and most tips can be utilized in a preventive maintenance plan for various family challenges. You may find something for a teenager that would be helpful for your 8-year-old and vice versa. Take what you like for your specific situation. As with most things in life, moderation is the key. As you read this book, the letters CEO will refer to Chief Executive Officer, as it was originally developed in the business world. However, other times CEO will be used in the context of Constantly Evaluating Others, which I have created. As you may know, I feel ALL moms held (and still hold) the first CEO title. As the reader, you can interchange them. And as I always say, "Parenting is tough, but don't forget the humor and never underestimate the power of prayer."

1 | Golden Rule Number One for Family Success:

Treat your children the way you want to be treated.

What is preventive maintenance? For our cars, it's an oil change done on a regular basis. As long as it takes place close to the scheduled time in the owner's manual, it usually helps keep the car in good running order. This is one example of a preventive maintenance plan. There are no manuals, instructions or schedules that are given to us as parents. We have to come up with our own preventive maintenance plan to keep our children in "good running order" (not to mention to keep our sanity). Monkey see, monkey do! Always remember that little eyes and ears are all around us taking in everything we do. Sooner or later they will do and say exactly what others in the family have done. This means you. Tune in to your tone of voice. If you bark commands, children will learn to bark back! Parents and caregivers are children's best teachers. Teach them acceptable thoughts, words and behaviors that will lead to mutual respect.

QUESTION: How is the best way for a parent to handle his/her behavior during stressful situations with children at home?

A. Even though you may feel like screaming, keep your voice low in stressful situations. Tune in to your tone of voice. Try to avoid blowing your top. Practice active listening and if you feel like you are going to explode, it may help to leave the room, count to ten, say a prayer or take a walk. You may need to do all of the above. Tell your children you need to leave the room for your own "time out," but that you will be right back. Depending on your children's ages and the specific situation, a timer or stop watch may need to be used to let them know how long you will be gone. Set it for a certain amount of time and put it in plain sight where it can be seen. If you can take only five minutes, so be it. It's better than nothing. Check a clock or watch to make sure you know when the timer will go off. Go into another area and close the door. Look right into the mirror and say all the things you wished you could say directly to them. This is a great stress buster. It works wonders for "telling off" others as well: a spouse, sister, boss, etc.

B. Pop in a CD. Keep a CD or cassette player set up in your time-out spot. Maybe even use a computer to help you with music choices or playing CDs. Play your favorite music and take a break from the situation. Focus on the music — it can completely change your attitude. Be a little daring by dancing or singing along. There's a little bit of musical talent in all of us. If not, fake it.

C. Plan ahead. If your children are crying and screaming and will not calm down, try to step out of the room and take a quick break. Do it for yourself as well as for them. If there is another adult around, ask him or her to watch the kids while you take a little longer break.

Make up a phrase or a signal to let your spouse or other adult know when you need to take a break. Try saying "TIME OUT FOR ME" while pointing to yourself — it will make it clear you need time away from the situation now! If weather permits, take a walk. Take music with you or sing your own songs while walking. If there's no one else in the house and you need to get out, call a friend or neighbor. Responsible teenagers can also help out. Keep a list of babysitters by the phone and the best time to reach them — and call them. Or trade off with a friend you know will be home who can run over and help watch the kids for a few minutes while you gather your thoughts.

D. Try the unexpected with your children. Get silly! Release tension by singing your answers or requests to your children. For example, when my children begin to complain and cry I sing the "Waa-Waa" song. Sing it to familiar tunes while imitating facial expressions of a not-so-happy camper. March in place, swing your arms and smile. Yes, I said smile! Since there is only one phrase in the song, "waa-waa," keep repeating it over and over to the same tune. The kids can't help but laugh, and before long they may join in. While everyone is having fun and calming down, their self-esteem is building. This off the wall approach implies that it's OK to vent angry feelings as long as no one gets hurt. It even provides an acceptable way to release pent-up energy. The child's self-worth has not been damaged because she feels comfortable enough to voice her opinion. Best of all it shows everything is not as serious as previously thought, and it sends a clear message that it's OK to laugh at yourself. So what if it sounds goofy; it works!

E. Stop talking and let your fingers do the work. Write notes to your children. Stick them up where they will be noticed and read. A teacher told me she clipped one of my Parent to Parent newspaper columns and mailed it to her teenager. He never learned where it came from and thought one of his friends or teachers was trying to tell him something. He got the message, and since his mother never mailed him letters she was never suspected of sending it. If your children can't read, draw a picture. Most children know what the happy face and the unhappy face look like. They will surely ask you about it. Or sit down and write out your feelings in a letter to yourself — or it can be addressed to the one who is upsetting you. This is for you to keep or throw away. It really might make you feel better. I love to sit down and color. And sure, I use my kids' crayons. There are such cool colors out today that it's fun to color in their coloring books. Turn on some of your favorite music and color away; let all the tension and frustrations flow out. Or if you prefer, use watercolors to vent and calm down. Go ahead, try some of these "no-brainers." There's a big kid inside all of us.

Motivating Kids for Positive Cooperation:

1. Set up a preventive maintenance plan with family rules and motivate the kids for positive cooperation. Provide choices and chances by issuing warnings. For children under the age of three, redirect their actions: Show them something else to do or play. Let's be honest here — redirecting attention works with most kids as well as most adults. Be realistic with kids: Don't threaten to do something you can't fulfill. For example, if you ground your children for two weeks and they're already driving you nuts, how can you keep them around for two weeks without going completely mad? Be sure to think before you speak!

2. Ask your kids non-threatening, open-ended questions to keep the lines of communication open. Try not to blame or point a finger before finding out the details. The situation may not be the way it seems. A good rule of thumb: We're all innocent until proven guilty.

3. Do not ask your children to do something you would not do yourself. How many times have you heard this? Put yourself in their shoes. Would you feel comfortable doing what you ask? Don't think that because they're kids they should do as you say if you're not setting a good example yourself. Get real and they will respect you for it.

4. Always say "please," "thank you" and "you're welcome." This teaches mutual respect and helps to develop respect toward others as well as personal self-worth. Showing respect to others is especially important to middle school kids and teenagers. Even thought they may act like they don't want respect or even need it from "their parents," they really do. Even with babies we can practice gestures along with words. Talk to your baby. Soon they will respond and make sounds back. This is their first introduction to communication outside the womb.

5. If something isn't working right away, do not panic or give up. Changing a habit is a major redo. Everyone, including yourself, is sometimes resistant to change. Your family team deserves your patience and understanding if you want these traits modeled back to you. Remember that a family team is made up of two or more people. Good parenting skills made better takes time. Begin slowly and take bits and pieces. Repetition while staying calm is the key to change.

TIPS (Tuned-In Parents Sharing)

QUESTION: How should I tell my child to handle bullies?

ANSWER: If you advise your child to hit back, it could be more trouble than what it is worth. We should not be encouraging our children to handle situations with violence. An eye for an eye is wrong. When this happened in our family, we told our child to give back what was received. The problem? We parents were battling it out for weeks while the kids got over it in a matter of seconds. This definitely made for an uncomfortable relationship with my neighbors. Also, parents need to consider whether or not their child is willing to accept responsibility for his or her actions. It may feel good to get anger out, but in may not be worth the consequences. - C.

A professional shares: Teach your child to first use all measures of assistance and reason to stop the bullying behavior, particularly if it is physical and could be harmful. Sometimes reasoning doesn't immediately work with bullies. Tell your child that it's a good idea to involve an authority figure: a parent, bus driver, teacher, etc. If the situation continues, teach your child how to protect himself. When confronted, bullies will often run away or find another outlet for their behavior. - Dr. Keith Dewey

Mommy–CEO, adding wisdom: In today's society and with the recent school shootings across the country, we have to take taunting and hitting seriously. Unfortunately, bullies will always be around — so get ready. Talk about the best way to handle various situations. If physical contact is involved, it's best to go straight to an authority figure. Teach your child it's not silly to voice his concerns. When the occasion arises, talk and role-play with your child. Let your child be the bully during role play. Find out where and when the bullying is taking place. Who is around? What is happening? These questions will help you gather details and help your child shed some of the emotions he is feeling.

Discuss the situation with your child's teachers. Make them aware of what is taking place and that you are serious about getting it to stop. Bullies are pretty slick and know exactly when to stir things up. The bullying may be verbal or physical; either way, it hurts and can damage self-esteem (and a lot more, if left to some kids). If you do not get the results you want, talk to the principal.

Signs that your child may be bullied — and in an uncomfortable situation — include torn clothes, slipping grades, upset stomach before school, requests for more lunch money or the inability to sleep at night. Many schools have implemented programs to help alleviate the stress and challenges that fighting and bullying can cause students, teachers and parents. I also recommend a favorite book about put-downs and teasing for children ages 4 to 8: *Simon's Hook* by Karen Gedig Burnett.

QUESTION: How do other mothers handle that crazy first hour right after getting home from work?

ANSWER: Even though I have things I need to get done at home or I'm stressed out and would rather be left alone for a while to unwind, I know that it will make for a much easier and happier evening for everyone if I just give them my undivided attention. It usually doesn't take a whole hour because if I really pay attention to them and talk with them, they feel secure again and will go play. The first thing we do is exchange kisses and hugs and sit down for a snack and let them tell me about their day. Sometimes we play a short game. If I try to cut this time short, they seem to just end up fighting and trying to get my attention anyway. Face it: if your kids need attention, they are going to get it one way or another. - Brandi

Mommy–CEO, adding wisdom: Anytime you have been away from the kids for several hours, they will once again need reassurance of your love and interest in them as individuals. This is true for all children, including teens. Here are some other things to try: Turn off any noise — TV, radio, computer, etc. — and sit down with them so you're on the same eye level for better eye contact. If you are feeling rushed because of an activity that the children are due to be at soon after you arrive home, at least take a few minutes to sit down and explain the situation.

Encourage them to continue to talk while getting ready. Let each child have a turn telling about his day without any interruptions. To keep things fair, remember who talked first the previous time. Let them take turns from day to day on who gets to talk first. Stories may have to be continued in the car. Repeat parts of what they say back to them (this is an important "parent test").

Don't be afraid of sharing about your day. If you've had a bad day, it's OK for them to know this. Consider the age of the child as to the depth of your explanation and try to end on a positive note. This is a golden rule of thumb even with teenagers. They just need to know things will work out and they don't need to worry about your situation.

QUESTION: My mother-in-law says I will spoil my newborn son if I don't stop holding him so much. Is this true?

ANSWER: You can't spoil a baby. If he could talk and could say, "Mommy, I'm overtired, cold, and I wish you would just hold me," would you answer, "No"? Your baby is communicating through various cries, and you will learn to interpret each kind: hungry, wet, tired, cold, pain or just needs human touch. Tell your mother-in-law that what worked well for her may not work well for your children — and you are comfortable holding your precious newborn. Use your instincts and common sense. - K. H.

ANSWER: This ages-old mother-in-law wisdom needs to be hung out to dry. While you could hold your baby too much and never get anything done, more than likely the baby has need of Mommy. I am the mother of six children. They are not babies anymore, but even some of the bigger ones still want to be held — and I hold them. As they get older, they want to be held less often. But I enjoy it all the same and am the one who wants to hold them longer. - Cynthia

ANSWER: I couldn't agree more with the parents. Be an advocate for your baby and cuddle as much as possible. Try new areas to kiss as well. The top of the head and the back of the neck are good ones and sometimes forgotten. - Dorothy

Mommy–CEO, adding wisdom: It's been proven over and over again that it's almost impossible to spoil a baby under the age of 12 months. In fact, babies who have to stay in a crib, playpen or swing and encounter a variety of babysitters day in and day out will be the ones crying more often and needing your attention longer. By holding the baby, you are encouraging a loving relationship and building his self-confidence, self-esteem and trust. In fact, I carried my children around in an infant carrier for as long as possible. I got plenty of household chores done and never heard a whimper. If he gets the attention he needs now, he will be much more independent as he gets older. At around 6 months old and depending on the situation, you might be able to entertain him by just being near. Try talking, playing or singing while sitting on the floor beside his crib. If he continues to cry, remember to check the temperature of his room. Is he over- or underdressed? Is his diaper wet? Go ahead and pick him up. You may wonder, Is he never to be held again as the years pass? Not! My youngest just turned 10 and he still loves to get big hugs while we sit on the couch and watch a movie.

QUESTION: How do I cope with my younger child's jealously of my older child's accomplishments?

ANSWER: We ran into this, and it can become an uphill battle. Parents need to be sure to concentrate on the various activities that the other child does well. Find out what the child excels at and make the most of it. I believe all children are gifted but not in the same way. We should all share and appreciate what is good in all of them. - Joan

A professional shares: When a child is jealous of an older sibling, he may be feeling discouraged and fearful that he is not unique and lovable to his parents. The child may persist in these beliefs in spite of evidence to the contrary and in spite of parents' attempts to convince him otherwise. At these times, focus on finding ways to support the younger child's self-confidence and growing sense of competence without becoming embroiled in a battle with the child over his jealousy. It is helpful to acknowledge the child's efforts and strengths and encourage continued positive efforts. Try to find a specific activity or interest area to focus on with the younger child. This will help the child establish an identity for himself as competent in that area. It is very important at these times to avoid criticism as much as possible. Try to focus on the positives. It is helpful for parents to arrange to spend specific individual times on a regular basis with the child who is unhappy and jealous. - Dr. Locke

Mommy–CEO, adding wisdom: All children are gifted in many different ways. In working with special education students, I even found it to be true there. Some mentally, emotionally and physically handicapped children could draw anything of interest to them or sculpt a piece of clay into a figure of perfection. Others could recite a lengthy poem word for word yet could not ever get their ABC's in the correct order. These kids, like "normal" kids, whatever that is, had numerous talents from which to draw. The real challenge was to find them and put them in the spotlight as often possible. I had one little boy who was very jealous of his older sibling. When we discovered that he had a nice singing voice and gave him an opportunity to use it often, he stopped most of his arguments at home. Hitting his older brother diminished within a few months. Find anything the jealous child does well and try to build on it for a lasting foundation, but always be sincere.

QUESTION: My son complains of his teacher being mean. How should I approach this?

ANSWER: The same thing happened with our daughter in kindergarten. We found out after the school year was over that she was right. Talk to other parents who have children in this teacher's class. Do they support what your son is saying? If so, take action. Even if your son merely says, "I think my teacher is mean," validate his opinion and find out why he is saying this. It may be a personality conflict that needs to be worked out. - A. K.

ANSWER: My granddaughter went through something similar. There was poor communication between her teacher and the family. We finally figured out the teacher was just simply tired of teaching and was burned out. We tried to impress upon our grand-daughter to try and turn the tables with kindness. She got her homework in on time and tried to keep a neat desk. She gave the teacher compliments, wrote her poems, colored seasonal pictures for her and always kept honesty on her side. The teacher's disposition never changed. But it taught our granddaughter not to expect people to change if they just don't want to — and to make the most out of a bad situation by staying positive herself - A.

ANSWER: It could be an oversight. I would suggest for you to go to the teacher and talk with her. She may be unaware of what is going on. I always appreciated any parent who came to me first with a problem. It allowed us to try and work things out together. - Ann H.

Mommy–CEO, adding wisdom: It sounds as if you may need to ask your son a few questions and write down his answers. Ask him in what way is the teacher mean? Is she mean to all the children? When does this usually happen — in the morning or afternoon? Does she ever smile? Does she ever laugh? Reverse roles and let him be the teacher and you the student. Ask for an example of each question. If you feel there's a need to get more answers, call for an appointment with the teacher. Try to make it during the time she has the children go to the library or do another activity. Talk with her in private. Try to stay around when the children come back to class. Watch how she relates to the class as a whole. Check with other parents. Have they heard similar comments at home from their children? The best way to get to know your child's teacher is to volunteer in the classroom. This will give you firsthand information on your child, and a bird's-eye view of how the whole classroom interacts as a group.

QUESTION: When I breastfeed my newborn, my preschooler becomes upset. What are ways to calm her down?

ANSWER: Develop an environment of normalcy for breastfeeding. Try to do it at a regular time, a regular way and a regular place, and do not become upset if your preschooler does. Use it as a time to teach her about proper parenting and the needs of newborns. Sometimes, older children feel their own security needs are not being met or recognized. Keep reassuring the preschooler of your love, and provide time to do things exclusively with her. - K. D.

ANSWER: When I was a little girl, my mom brought home a new baby brother. As soon as she stepped in the door with the new baby, she asked me to sit down and placed a pillow on my lap and let me hold him. This made me feel important, and she let me "help" often. If she was feeding him or just wanted to take him for a stroll in the stroller, I was often included and always thought I was a big help. - C. Becker

Mommy–CEO, adding wisdom: While the baby is sleeping, talk to your preschooler about the new baby and some of his needs while holding her in your lap. There are several books on this topic and most hospitals offer a new-sibling "before-and-after" class. Show and tell the older daughter how important she is to the newborn. Tape a few favorite songs sung by the preschooler and play them for the newborn. Hang pictures on the wall the older child colored and show the baby how good a job his or her big sister did. Let her pick out a few picture frames for her room and the nursery. Put a picture of the baby in her room and a picture of herself in the baby's room. Make a point to show the children each other's pictures and say things like, "Here's the new baby who needs a big sister's help." After a few weeks, put pictures of the two of them together in new frames. Let the preschooler help pick out the baby's toys and clothes. All these things might alleviate the "left out" feelings.

QUESTION: What is the best way to get my 11-year-old son interested in reading?

ANSWER: Children learn by our example, so parents who read are more likely to have children who read. An 11-year-old boy will be especially encouraged if his father is an avid reader. A child who is a good reader but who doesn't care to read might need help finding some books that are interesting to him. Check out the library or go to a bookstore and look for topics he is interested in. It might be fun for him to receive a gift certificate that he could use at a bookstore. That way, he could select and buy a book for himself. - Jenifer

ANSWER: Begin to read to them when they are young. As they grow, there are other ways to fuel their interest in reading: Clip magazine and newspaper articles you think will be of interest. Subscribe to age-appropriate magazines. Participate in reading programs through schools and the public library. Books containing endless sports statistics are also popular. Keep books on tape in the car. Discuss current affairs with your child. My son recently saw cloning featured on the cover of a magazine. Because he didn't fully understand the concept, it held an interest for him after seeing it on the news, and he asked if he could buy a copy of the magazine. My journalism students, who are voracious readers, said positive experiences have always come out of reading. Having their own library card and being able to read the authors they liked really seemed to encourage them. They suggested that parents and teachers should never use reading as punishment. As parents, we set aside time for sports, music lessons, homework and a multitude of other activities for our children. It is a thoughtful parent who sets aside time for their kids to develop a pleasure that will last forever. - Pamela

Mommy–CEO, adding wisdom: I agree. Begin to read to your children as soon as you can. As they get older, let them help pick out the books to be read and let them read to you. It's enjoyable for some children to read to other siblings. If your children are old enough to share in this activity, offer it as a choice at least once a week. As with many things in life, sometimes an activity loses its appeal — so letting someone different do it may create new inspiration. Or it may just look that way. For example, I've noticed that on some days my children are eager to read in the evenings, while on other days it can become a power struggle (which can turn into a nightmare). I've had to learn to become more tuned in to their moods and go with the flow. Turning them off from reading is the last thing I want to happen. It's not going to kill any of us if they skip a night or two. In fact, sometimes I enjoy and need a break just as much as they do.

QUESTION: How do you keep things "fair" for kids who are always comparing how much each one gets?

ANSWER: My husband and I sat down with our three kids and explained that we "owed" and would provide for them adequate shelter, food and clothing; would teach them right from wrong; and would offer an appropriate education along with plenty of love. Everything else was "gravy" and would be dished out as we saw fit. From that day forward, they got what we thought each needed. Sometimes one would get more or less than the other two. Things pretty much even out over time. If any arguing occurred about feeling shortchanged, they would be taken out of an activity and be banished to their room for at least two hours. For an argument over an item, we would take it away to never be given back again. - J. B.

ANSWER: It is important to teach children that everything is not always fair. We used to shop for our clothing in secondhand stores. When one of the children complained that the other sibling got more clothing or other items, I would tell them that some days I just found more things that suited or fit one child more than the other. The next time we went shopping, we might find lots of things that fit the other. Once they grasped that concept, it was smooth sailing. - Brenda

ANSWER: The way I approach this is with the knowledge that life is not always fair, and the sooner children learn this the better. My grandchildren have come to accept that each one is treated according to the particular situation on that particular day, and that I have my reasons if someone gets a toy and another does not. They seem to respect this once they get beyond the initial complaint. It also fosters good behavior — and then I don't mind giving a special treat. - Toni

ANSWER: I have three boys. One day I found out that the timer on a microwave, a cuckoo clock or an egg timer works wonders. No matter if it's Nintendo, the computer, the trampoline or whatever, using a timer is always fair. Nobody in my house argues when it rings, beeps or chimes because it is an object. It's simple, inexpensive and settles every argument. Even time-out is not a problem anymore. - Angela

Mommy–CEO, adding wisdom: From a very early age, children are taught to be fair in sharing, caring and taking turns. As they get older, it becomes a real issue to their integrity and self-esteem that they are treated fair out of simple respect. It can quickly get out of hand as they approach early elementary age. By first grade, they need to become more aware of things working out for the best in the end for everyone. To end current battles, make a chart with each child's name on it and add a check for each time something is bought. Leave spaces for the reason why: baseball — a glove; soccer – a pair of shoes; church choir — a dress. Don't record the price, for this will lead to questions about fairness in the amount of money spent. The chart will help everyone see who got what last — and why. After a while, you will no longer need the chart.

QUESTION: Our 4-year-old daughter carries her blankie everywhere. What's a good way to wean her of it?

ANSWER: After telling your daughter you'd like to wean her away from her blankie, wait a few days to let the idea sink in. Begin by cutting it in half. Sew and finish the edges of one half and tell her it is her "at home" blanket. Use the other half to make a large pocket on a garment, or a scarf, hat, vest or stuffed animal. Let her choose. She can now leave the house with her blankie, but it will be in one of these items. She will still have the tactile security of her blanket. - Carl

ANSWER: After losing it, we replaced our son's cherished blankie with a new one. Now we have a rule that he can take it with him as long as it remains in the van when we reach our destination. We also told him it was his responsibility to remember everything he wanted to take with him. If he forgot it, he had to tough it out. He gradually has started leaving it at home. He takes it with him to bed at night or to take a nap. - Pam

ANSWER: Your 4-year-old feels insecure. Her blanket makes the world a less terrifying place. She may give it up eventually, but when she is ready and not because you want her to. Let her have it. It is only a small thing that makes her happy. - Darla

Mommy–CEO, adding wisdom: Under stress, children react to situations in various ways. Stressful situations may be moving, a new sibling, divorcing parents or a death in the family. Children need a sense of security. It might be a beloved blankie or another item. Just go with the flow. Don't let comments of family or friends pressure you into a frustrating confrontation with your 4-year-old. There are bigger battles on the horizon.

Mommy–CEO for Family Success on Golden Rule One:

As a parent or caregiver, you are not perfect and should not expect your children to be. Try to manage your family team creatively. Get started on a preventive maintenance plan for your family and consider implementing

some of the skills shared. Displaying personal acceptable behavior for your team members to model will put you on the right track as one of your top goals for preventive maintenance. This will be a positive direction, which  may ensure family success. It will allow you to build their self-esteem while teaching and sharing mutual respect. Parents and caregivers "Constantly Evaluate Others" along with the options to help guide the family team with the best information for their daily choices. Provide choices and let them choose. Tune in to your tone of voice and monitor your personal actions.

TREAT CHILDREN THE WAY YOU WANT TO BE TREATED.

A Little Evaluation:

LOVE YOUR CHILDREN EACH DAY

Love and care for your children,

they never get too big for a hug.

Give them the time they deserve from you,

the years they are small are few,

Let them help in the kitchen,

teach them how to bake,

and don't fret over the mess, for Heaven's sake!

Let them get their fingers gooey and
lick clean the spoon,

for in a few years they'll be leaving — all far too soon.

Read many stories and sing a lot of songs,

for they'll have their own type of music
before too long.

Teach them how to give and share,

let them respect those with handicaps,

and, politely not to stare.

Let them help themselves whenever they can,

responsibilities help them become
a better woman or man.

Remind yourself daily that they mimic
what they hear and see,

and last but not least,

Teach them about God — this is my final plea.

Notes

_____

_____

_____

_____

_____

_____

_____

_____

_____

_____

_____

_____

_____

_____

_____

_____

_____

_____

_____

2 | GOLDEN RULE Number Two for Family Success:

Know your children's ages and stages.

Whether your children are 2 weeks old or 18 years old, as the CEO of your family team, it is your responsibility to educate yourself on the developmental ages and stages of your children. Taking the time to tune in and to learn about your children's individual ages and stages will be one of the most important things you can do for a solid preventive maintenance plan for family success. Find out about their physical, emotional and mental capabilities. Many parenting magazines as well as many websites are now offering this as a regular feature in their child development sections. This is fantastic. However, to get a more in-depth look, consider utilizing tapes, books, CDs or television programs. This will help immensely in having realistic expectations of what children can and want to do.

For example, if you find your 7-year-old cooperative and happy as can be one day and the next day — or even a few hours later — has turned a 90-degree angle in personality, it's time to go get information on 7-year-olds. Remember, books or other information will not match and "size-up" your child perfectly or totally. Don't expect this. It's not healthy for anyone to expect magical conclusions; we are all different. What you might find is being happy one minute and extremely sad the next is normal behavior for most children this age. The source (book or whatever) should explain these emotions. The enlightenment and options discovered will arm you with information and under-standing to build a better working relationship with your family team. (Not to mention to stop you from running outside and screaming in front of all the neighbors). Keep it simple. Do not analyze and agonize over every detail. These are approximate guidelines and all children will not fit every example. But learning more about your children's ages and stages does help — and most of the time makes sense.

QUESTION: Why does my child "act out" so often with unacceptable behavior?

A. Watch his behavior in different situations. Is there something in particular that is causing him to become frustrated? I remember one year when my 6-year-old would become very upset and display unacceptable behavior toward me and other family members. This happened after every soccer practice. It was apparent to me that this sport he loved so much was taking a toll on him, as well as the rest of us. I soon narrowed it down to the exact action — or lack thereof — which was causing the problem. As soon as the coach asked the kids to dribble the ball down the field, he would panic. In talking with him, I found out he felt awkward because he couldn't keep up with some of the other children and didn't feel good about his performance. Letting him know this was something we could work on at home, and giving him the choice to make the decision about doing it, worked out great. A few extra practices in our backyard gave him the self-esteem and encouragement he needed to try to become better when asked to perform on the field.

B. Even though the Internet is helpful, books allow you to make notes to refer to at a later date and to carry them with you (although I know we will be holding the Internet in our hands by the time this book is finished). Books are totally different and I think you know what I mean. Go to the bookstore and purchase a book covering the ages of your children. Is the child 2 years old and trying to assert himself as an individual? (NEWSFLASH — Stock up on upset-stomach medicine.) This asserting bit happens again during various ages and stages throughout childhood, including the preteen and teenage years. I cannot stress how important it is to learn about our children's ages and stages. Are you sick of hearing this? Good! I've done my job.

It is appalling to me to see how many parents just will not listen to this advice. Once you begin reading about each child, things will click and many answers may become crystal clear. It will astonish and amaze you at how accurate most of the information will seem. You may be reading and thinking at the same time, "Oh, so that's why 10-year-olds don't especially like to brush their teeth!" Remember, don't take any book too literally, and use it only as a guideline. Your children may be ahead or behind the suggestions in the book or chart. Look at this word again: "suggestions." Everyone has something to tell you: doctors, teachers, grandparents, relatives and neighbors — just keep their comments as suggestions and not as rules. After you find the right book, put it in a place where you can refer to it often. Sometimes while rereading it, which you should do every three to four months, a whole different perspective will form. If your child appears to be behind, don't panic or become upset or sad.

After having three kids of my own and raising my little sister (yes, that makes FOUR) I've come to terms with reality: children are individuals and develop at different rates. The outcome is that almost everyone catches up and levels out by the second or third grade. Girls have a tendency to be a little ahead of the game in most early developmental tasks.

C. Don't label your child! After becoming educated on your child's ages and stages, consider what has happened in the past and tune in to what is happening now. This may help to explain some questions and prevent many hardships on the success of the family team. It will also keep you on track with realistic expectations. Make sure you do not tag your child with a label of any kind. If your child displays a behavior that you do not agree with, don't say, "You're bad!" If you label a child, he will begin to see himself as being that way. Take a few minutes and think about it. Like most of us, if he constantly hears, "You are so slow!" eventually he would have no other choice but to believe it. The labels and words become self-fulfilling prophecies. A child will try to fulfill the expectations adults have set up. This is true for all of us. On the other side of the coin, if you constantly say "Good boy!" or "Good girl!" your child can encounter a different type of failure in another unhealthy role. A feeling of having to always be good or even perfect may evolve, wherein making a mistake could be devastating. There is great fear of tarnishing the role he has been placed in, and it is a very scary feeling. Instead of labeling him, talk about the behavior. Tell him he is displaying "unacceptable behavior." Don't forget to notice the display of acceptable behavior by saying, "You should be very proud of yourself! Good job!" These words, said with a smile and a thumbs-up gesture, will let him know you are very proud, too!

D. Ask other people about what's going on. Now is not the time to be reserved. If he attends school, childcare, nursery school, a mother's-day-out program, preschool, or just plays in a playgroup, ask other people if they have noticed any strange or unusual behavior. If so, when does it happen? If the child is older, ask his friends if they've noticed why he becomes upset. What is he doing at the time and who is he around? Don't forget to stop and tune in to your own attitude regarding certain situations. Are you sending over-anxious or frustrated feelings to your family? Do you have too much on your plate? If so, take time to keep something going on in your personal life that you really enjoy. Do something for yourself that helps you relax and build your self-esteem without making you feel guilty.

Motivating Kids for Positive Cooperation:

1. Have positive expectations for your children's behavior by staying positive yourself. Tune in to your tone of voice and monitor your body language. Having a positive outlook will help introduce a preventive maintenance plan to your family team. Take a little time for yourself.

2. Solve problems together and offer choices. Let the kids come up with some ideas on discipline challenges. You may not agree with them, but they will feel much better about being heard. And who knows? It may be something that can be used. Kids can come up with some pretty good rules.

3. Let children air their feelings. Reverse roles. Tune in and listen to their viewpoints. It may help you to understand them better as individuals. For younger children, help them channel their feelings into nondestructive and acceptable actions. Buy a lightweight ball they can kick far. Let them run after it and kick it again. This is a great way of releasing angry feelings. Let older children exert energy by kneading bread dough. Who knows? They may even become interested in baking!

4. Be flexible. Don't be a constant pushover, but it really is OK to change your mind in a situation every once in a while. If you see a family rule or plan is just not going to work because of ages, stages or a situation, change it for now. Don't be afraid to admit mistakes. This is a normal sign of being truthful and setting a good example for family members.

5. Use a timer. Set a timer for a certain amount of minutes to get something done. This works well for young to middle-age children. Help them to get started on their task. Kids are usually more cooperative if an adult pitches in and helps them begin a project. Parents can make a difference.

TIPS (Tuned-In Parents Sharing)

QUESTION: What are the best ways of handling a temper tantrum?

ANSWER: A technique I used as a dental hygienist is very effective. When a child begins to lose control, I lean down right next to the child's ear and place my hands on her shoulders or hug her (whichever is appropriate), and speak calmly into her ear. I say, "You can't hear what I am saying when you scream, cry and yell like this. You need to quiet down so you can hear me." Say this over and over. Never raise your voice or get into a shouting match. This will only escalate the child's behavior and frustration level. Try to maintain eye contact and keep your voice low. - Leann

ANSWER: We threw the words "I promise" out the window. If we told our daughter we promised to do something and it didn't work out, we got the fuel going for a fire. And we had plenty of sparks! We changed our wording to "We will try to go to the park," instead of "We promise." We went further to explain how maybe the day looked really busy and we might not have time for certain things. If we let her know ahead of time that an event may not happen, it worked wonders. - John and Anne

Mommy–CEO, adding wisdom: This is a big deal with many families, especially when taking small children shopping. Here are a few pointers: If your child has just been at preschool or childcare, she's probably tired. Even though she may have enjoyed her day, her energy level may be depleted. If she's screaming about something, it's probably just you she really needs. Try to do errands later and just go home for now. If errands can't be avoided, plan ahead and take a special toy or book from home to be used in the store. After arriving home, put the special thing up and out of sight until the next trip. Or offer another option: Let her help you "buy" something. Let her hold lightweight items and put them in the cart. Don't begin your sentence with "No!" Instead, say, "We cannot buy it today," and keep your tone calm. With older children, make an offer to put an item on their birthday or Christmas list. Keep a notepad with you at all times and let them see you write the item on the list. Elementary school kids can write it down on the list themselves when they get home and even begin saving up for it.

QUESTION: How can we help our 4-week-old with colic?

ANSWER: Our old vacuum cleaner saved our sanity during the last week of our daughter's colic. I placed her up high so her stomach lay flat on my shoulder, switched on the vacuum cleaner and slowly vacuumed the whole house for hours and hours. I even figured out how to read a book during these sessions by wedging a paperback between my thumb and the vacuum handle. - Amy

ANSWER: Our daughter had colic and we found noise helped her the most. We also found a cassette tape — also offered on CD — called "For Crying Out Loud," by The Right Start. It can be ordered by calling 1-800-548-8531. It is a recording of eight sounds to calm your baby: maternal heartbeat, car wipers, rain, blow dryer, vacuum cleaner, restaurant ambiance, washing machine and waves on a beach. - P. J.

ANSWER: Our tap water contained liberal amounts of minerals. Our pediatrician recommended that we only use distilled water for our baby's formula and drinking water. Make sure it is not plain bottled water — it must say "distilled" on the label. - Jane

ANSWER: We switched our baby formula to a protein base and this made all the difference. During feedings or whenever the baby cries, place a warm, wet cloth on her tummy. Moms need to also remember that things are less hectic and stressed if they are getting their own rest. - L.

ANSWER: Try a can of soymilk for babies. If there's no discomfort, this is the answer. It's easier and a lot cheaper. Our children used it and many of our friends used it as well. - George

ANSWER: Our baby stopped crying when we placed her a baby swing. It worked wonderfully and she spent many happy hours swinging. - Elizabeth

ANSWER: My baby had a very bad case of colic. One day I was rocking him and playing with the motor from my breast pump. I turned it on and he stopped crying! It worked every time. - Debbie

ANSWER: We switched form regular bottles to the Playtex Nurser with disposable bags. As the baby fed, we pinched the bottom of the bag until all the air was out and the formula was coming out the top. He got all formula and no air. It was more expensive and time consuming, but well worth it for everyone. - Pam

Mommy–CEO, adding wisdom: Many moms say that breastfed babies usually don't have colic. I breastfed two of my children and while colic was very limited, they still had it for around 60 days. I do support breastfeeding as the best method for any baby. There's plenty of help available through various support groups. Remember to check with your pediatrician or pharmacist if you have a concern with any of the remedies listed above. Some doctors don't agree with over-the-counter solutions, but ask about them anyway. If after discussing the topic with your doctor and finding out they are not harmful to your baby and could possibly work, follow your gut instinct. One mom from New York wrote to say she sat the baby in the kitchen and let her faucet run over pans turned upside down. The odd noise was quite soothing. I had the most success with the washing machine. I put in a load of clothes and sat the baby on top of the washing machine in an infant seat. Make sure you securely hold onto the seat and never leave the baby unattended.

QUESTION: How can we teach our son to tie his shoes?

ANSWER: We worked on tying shoes the traditional way for about six to eight months. Then I remembered something an old friend had been taught by her parents: Make each lace one-half of a bow and tie them. All that children have to do is pull both bows to tighten. Also, use adult-size shoes (they have longer laces and are easier to maneuver for little fingers). Once they have mastered "big" shoes, children can work with their own. Do this without putting the shoes on but facing the proper way, and make a game of it. - Patti

ANSWER: Take a top lid of a shoebox and punch

holes in it to resemble a child's shoe. Run a shoelace through it. The child can then place the box in his lap and practice. I taught both of my children this way. - Lisa

ANSWER: Children learn to tie their shoes when a few basic criteria are met. First, when they develop small-muscle coordination. Second, when they have many opportunities to observe others tying shoes. Third, when they want to attempt tying their shoestrings in the presence of patient, encouraging adults. Children will learn to tie their shoes sometime between the ages of 4 and 7. - Cheryl

ANSWER: We taught our children how to tie their shoestrings by sitting behind them. They could see the correct direction of our fingers and shoestrings. - Ruthie

ANSWER: Get a long, flexible rope. (A jump rope will work.) Place the child on your lap facing forward. Help the child tie the rope in a large bow around his thigh. It's easy to master the mechanics of bow tying when the string is oversized. This knowledge is then easy to transfer to real shoelaces. - Kristie

ANSWER: Neither of my children was particularly good with their hands, so tying shoelaces was very frustrating. I found that by letting them work from the "end" back, they were guaranteed success. Let him do the last step, then the last two steps, and so forth. For my left-handed daughter, the key seemed to be having her left-handed teacher teach her. - Pat

Mommy–CEO, adding wisdom: To prevent frustration, do not try to teach a child younger than age 5. For most children, especially boys, the fine motor skills are just not developed. Teach in small time slots. The two of you could quite possibly be in tears if you don't take it a little at a time. Take the shoe off and place it on top of the table. Face it the correct way. This will offer plenty of time and flexibility in arm and finger space. Above all else, let someone else try to teach if a battle develops. Keep the process lighthearted and fun.

QUESTION: My 8-year-old is afraid of the dark. What can I do?

ANSWER: I found a colorful blanket that we used for picnics. I placed the blanket on our sons and said a prayer. It went something like this: "Oh, safe blanket, protect my sons from all evil and let them sleep in peace this night. Thank you and Amen." This worked like a charm for all three sons! - Dennis

ANSWER: Give your son a choice of a flashlight to tuck under his pillow or a bedside lamp he can control. This will enable him to be "in charge." - Jeanne H.

ANSWER: Why not try a cassette tape or CD of music he would enjoy listening to while in bed? I have a nightlight for my daughter and we play her choice of her favorite music. This keeps her busy listening, and by the time it is done, she more often than not goes to sleep. - Micky

ANSWER: When my daughter was young, she was afraid to shut off the lights because there were monsters in her closet and under her bed. I took an air freshener spray can, covered it in paper to make my own "Monster Spray." I'd spray the Monster Spray under her bed and in the closet, and she slept knowing they were gone. You might also try leaving a light on. After all, aren't we all afraid of the dark? - D.E.

Mommy–CEO, adding wisdom: We tried an idea from a mom who said she hung cool patio lights around her son's room. It creates a nice glow and all his friends thought it was awesome. Here are a few more things you might want to take a look at: How busy is the bedroom? Also, make a rule about caffeine and explain it to the child. For example, none is served after 6:00 p.m. This should include food that contains chocolate as well as drinks. Limiting certain videos, TV shows, computer games and movies right before bedtime could be another tactic. Roughhousing too close to bedtime seems to stimulate children instead of calming them down or "wearing them out," and scary stories will only add to the problem for some. Above all, don't make fun or dismiss this as being silly. Maybe share a personal story of you being scared as a child. This always seems to work wonders.

QUESTION: It's a big hassle for me to get my 9-month-old to eat meat — even though it's combined with fruit in baby food. What can I do?

ANSWER: First-time parents seem to be overly worried about this. Don't be. Babies will eat meat in their own good time. Protein and vitamins are in almost all other food sources. As long as the baby is getting enough of a variety of vegetables, fruits, rice and iron, there is no need for alarm. - J. D.

ANSWER: Today parents have a new choice, fruit-and-meat combinations. Our son did not like baby food that contained meats, and we did not force the issue. We fed him baby cereal and formula. It provided most of the protein and iron for the first year. Now, at the age of 3, he eats all types of meat. - Beth

A professional shares: An infant can receive adequate protein and iron from formula with iron. By the time the baby is 9 months, try mixing a little broth with baby food. The salt and texture has basically been removed from the baby food bought from the store. Try offering the baby home-cooked casseroles, cheese, or well-cooked meats served or cut into small portions. Offer them in limited portions and sparingly. Breastfed babies need more protein a little earlier, and your pediatrician can help you with a plan for this. - Dr. Veerkamp

Mommy–CEO, adding wisdom: I breastfed two of my three children, and all three had a problem with food that contained meats. Here's what I did: I cooked my own meats and ground them up in a food processor. We couldn't afford the state-of-the-art kind, so I bought one of those simple "hand-held-crush-up" jars used for onions, pecans, etc. To make sure they ate at least some of the meat, I put pudding on the tip of the spoon along with a small amount of meat and salt, then sang, danced, laughed, clapped, and praised to encourage a laugh or smile. At the instance of that first smile or giggle, I quickly got a little bite in. After each bite, I began the whole scenario over again. I always acted like a big clown.

QUESTION: With all the "experts" arguing over the right age and time to potty train, when should we begin training our 2-year-old son?

ANSWER: When my grandson was little, his father was away much of the time in the service in Fort Campbell, Kentucky. So, when he was home, it was special and the little boy wanted to be just like his dad. He noticed his dad had fruit on the tag inside his "big boy" pants and liked that a lot. I got the idea to sew different pieces of fruit into his training pants so he felt he was important and a "big boy." To this day, you can still buy individual pieces of fruit from a fabric store. Just sew them into the back of plain white "big boy" pants. My little grandson never once wet his special training underwear because he was so proud to be like Dad! - Mrs. P.

ANSWER: We began training our son at the age of 2 years and 4 months. We overdid it at first, making him go too often, and he began to hate it and refused to go to the potty at all. A friend suggested food coloring. After he used the potty, we put in a drop of food coloring to see what color it would turn and he loved it! - Becky

ANSWER: I trained my daughter pretty quickly. The only thing I used was determination. I had one in diapers and the "new" baby was due soon. I couldn't bear the thought of having two in diapers. I sat her on the big toilet often and gave big hugs and lots of praise. - Josephine

ANSWER: Getting my 3-year-old son to go to the potty for wee-wee was not a problem. We used stars and prizes. It was when he needed to have a bowel movement that he demanded a diaper. I was so tired and exasperated after trying "everything" because nothing seemed to work. One day when he came to me for a diaper, out of total frustration I told him we were all out and we couldn't buy any more! He refused to go to the potty and held it in all day. Finally he raced for the potty and after he had success, we both danced for joy. That was it; just getting him to do it the first time was all it took. - Beth

ANSWER: We began potty training our son at the suggested age of 3 years. This went well in the beginning. But when it came to a bowel movement, he would always dirty his training pants. After a month of dirty underwear, we finally realized he would hide under or behind something. We soon learned to watch him and would immediately put him on the potty as soon as he hid under a table or behind a chair. Finally, he got the idea it was OK to use the potty for this purpose as well — and he never had another accident in his big-boy pants. - L. K.

ANSWER: Each child develops at a different rate. Do not feel pressured by friends and families who say their child was potty trained by 2. If your attempts are unsuccessful, postpone them until a later date. We found our 2-year-old son sitting on the big-boy potty because he wanted to please us. When we became upset and frustrated when he messed up his training pants, he became just as upset. In fact, he started hitting everyone in the family (including the pets). We stopped and tried again in six months. We put a potty outside where he played, and in no time he became potty trained. - B.A.

ANSWER: Make it kind of fun and not overwhelming. I put a potty in the bathroom when both my children were in diapers. They would both cart it around for a while and use it for a chair. This helped them to explore the "potty-chair." When they started showing signs of readiness for the potty, they would come get me or bring the potty to wherever I was. Don't rush your children by telling them what to do and how often. They will tell you; after all, it's their bodies and they know what their feelings are inside, not you. - Pat

ANSWER: We made two charts for our son, one for wee-wee and one for a bowel movement. We hung them up in the bathroom. We gave him a sticker and let him place it on the correct chart after each trip. For making a bowel movement in the potty (instead of his underwear) he got to choose Lego's, cars, motorcycles, trees, etc. This worked like a charm. We eventually stopped the rewards, but he still was very proud of himself and will occasionally still ask for a special sticker. - Elisabeth

ANSWER: The most important thing to remember when potty training is to recognize that each child is different and develops at a different rate. If one trained early, great! But don't expect it for the second, third, etc. Little children can be very stubborn and if you demand that they go potty, you will be the one who is surprised by the stress! Relax, don't worry about the "experts," and listen to your child. - Kristy

Mommy–CEO, adding wisdom: With today's busy families, the complete toilet learning process could take up to six months. It will begin with the child feeling the urge to go, being able to walk or run to the potty and pulling down his or her pants. Then he'll have to get the business done, use toilet paper (you'll help with this for a while), pull up his pants, flush the toilet and wash his hands. Learning and completing these steps before age 2 is considered early by most professionals, the "average" age being 36 months. Your child may begin learning by 20 months and others by 4 years. It all depends on the readiness of the child and his attitude. Of course, the time the parent, childcare provider or preschool teacher has to give, and their attitude, will play a big part in the process. Once he realizes he can control the adult, it becomes his ball game. For now, go with the flow, begin at around the age of 3 for boys and maybe 2 to 2 _ for girls (depending on the child). Children must be physically ready as well as mentally ready. If your child sits on the potty for wee-wee but still wears a diaper a night, he's not potty trained. To be physically ready, the sphincter muscles, which control all bowel and wee-wee movements, must be mature enough for the toddler to "stop and go potty." These sets of muscles seem to mature earlier in most girls than boys. Summertime may prove to be easier for training for many children and parents. Listen to your children and not your neighbors. Plan on at least one solid week of nothing but potty training to get a good, healthy start. Try not to use food as a bribe. Potty train outside if the weather permits — why not? The hose will provide an easy way to clean up the kids and any mess. Do not spank your children for mistakes. It will only backfire! If your ready and he's not, leave it be and come back to it later.

QUESTION: My preschooler bites other children in his class. What can I do?

ANSWER: Many preschool and childcare facilities have implemented a "three-bites-and-you're-out" policy. Try to correct the biting problem immediately. Here are a few suggestions: Explain to the child that biting is an unacceptable behavior. Place him in a time-out appropriate for his age (one minute for each year). Let him know you still love him but you do not like him to bite. After time-out, state again that it is not OK to bite and that if he doesn't stop, he may not get to come back to school and play with his friends. Give him a hug and send him on his way. - Barbara

ANSWER: I have four children and only one was a biter. Still, it was a big problem. We tried many things, including repeating over and over again: "Biting is not a nice feeling to the other child. It hurts!" But more than anything else, time and experience took care of it. As he grew, so did his understanding of the word "hurt." - Sue

Mommy–CEO, adding wisdom: While teaching preschool, I noticed one child was biting quite a bit. I found out he went to visit his father and a new baby stepbrother every other week. Another child in class had a new baby at home too, and seemed to get bit the most. The biter realized he did not get to see his family's new baby every day like his friend. I asked each child in the class to bring in a bear and a teething ring. The teething ring was tied to the bear's neck with a ribbon to make a necklace. I told them to offer the ring to the bear if they felt he was angry. I said he would be happy to share it with them if they felt the need to bite as long as they would give him a hug afterward. They liked this idea. The biting soon stopped and hugging became quite popular.

QUESTION: How's the best way to take away our almost-3-year-old's binky?

ANSWER: One of our friends told us to simply make a slice in the binky with a knife or scissors. This gives it a completely different sucking effect. It becomes no longer pleasurable. - Gayle

ANSWER: Don't be so concerned about such a soothing habit. Think of it along these terms: When was the last time you saw a child with a binky at kindergarten? Babies pace themselves and learn to substitute other activities for their needs. Consider some of the consequences or substitutes of forced withdrawal: hair sucking, finger chewing, nail biting and sucking on clothing. Give your child more time and ignore the comments of others. - Carol

ANSWER: We left it to Santa. We told our daughter he was going to give it to a baby who needed it because she didn't have one. She was very willing to do this because Santa left her a present with a special thank-you note. - Sue

ANSWER: My sister-in-law gave the best advice for how to take away a pacifier. It worked for her children and it also worked for mine. The best part was that all this was accomplished without tears or tantrums. In the first week, cut off the end of the binky. In the second week, take another little bit off. Continue this process until the binky becomes useless. Sooner or later, it will be left behind. - Linda

ANSWER: Don't rush your almost-3-year-old. We tried to take away our 3-year-old's binky, and he began to wet his pants (after being potty trained). At the age of 4, he gave it to the Tooth Fairy. She left him a note and asked for it. She was to give it to a new little baby. - E.

Mommy–CEO, adding wisdom: Many readers wrote in to tell me about cutting off the end of the binky or making a hole in it. My only hesitations are in creating a choking hazard with loose parts, and bacterial "stuff" getting caught inside the binky. Once cut, the pacifier nipple should immediately pop back into shape when firmly pulled. To prevent too many germs from collecting inside the pacifier, make this one a "just-inside-the-house" binky. If your child sticks everything into her mouth, chews and actually swallows, you might want to consider another option.

Remember, if your toddler is going through any type of a change that might be upsetting — a move, grandparents leaving, switching childcare or preschool teachers, a new baby in the house or a divorce — wait before making any changes. A pacifier brings pleasure and comfort, especially in stressful situations.

Mommy — CEO for Family Success on Golden Rule Two:

Whatever the ages of your children, find out what developmental stages they are going through. Learn enough to get through the present parenting challenge and then find the best way to handle the situation according to your children as individuals. After you work things out, find a leisurely time to regroup and review the information. Try to keep up with, or ahead of, develop- mental ages and stages for better parenting. As

Mommy!

the CEO of your family team, it is your responsibility to become a better tuned-in parent by educating yourself. This is an essential factor in a preventive maintenance plan for family success and to keep your team in "good running order."
Stop, look and listen.

KNOW YOUR CHILDREN'S AGES
AND STAGES.

A Little Evaluation:

Hey Mom — YOU KNOW
YOU'VE MADE A DIFFERENCE ...

WHEN:

One day you play catch with your children and the next evening at the ball field when one of the players ends up sick, your son volunteers you as a player.

WHEN:

Your child catches his first big fish and you're not around, but he asks the nearest neighbor to take a picture and shouts, "This will make a good surprise for my mom!"

WHEN:

Your children come running up to you and say, "Mom, which pair of shoes looks the best with this outfit?" (Because you know if you would have picked out the shoes beforehand, they would have surely turned up their noses and worn different ones.)

WHEN:

After taking out one of the kids for a fun-filled day, he buys gifts for the other siblings and surprises them upon returning home.

WHEN:

Everyone else at camp is making a yo-yo for himself and your child makes you a leather butterfly hairpin painted red, white and blue.

WHEN:

You run over an animal for the first time in your life and burst into tears — and the kids pat you on the back and say, "Mom, it's OK — at least you only hit one."

WHEN:

Your children save at least two quarters each week to put in the "Feed the Children" jars at local stores.

WHEN:

Your smallest son asks why you always pray at night for people who have kids — and then does it himself a few days later.

WHEN:

Your child is asked out of 150 other students to read a poem he wrote at a school graduation and dedicates it to you.

WHEN:

Your child tells a friend not to steal another child's toy by saying, "God will punish you, like you may be running and you might trip and hurt yourself really bad. That would be God teaching you a lesson."

WHEN:

Your kids run to give you a hug after being gone for a couple of nights.

WHEN:

Babysitters tell you to call anytime because your kids are a delight to be around.

WHEN:

You ask the question, "If you had three wishes, what would you wish for?" and the answer is world peace, no more hungry and homeless people, and a cure for all diseases. (God Bless America!)

Notes

_____

_____

_____

_____

_____

_____

_____

_____

_____

_____

_____

_____

_____

_____

_____

_____

_____

_____

3 | Golden Rule Number Three for Family Success:

Teach your children responsibility.

Responsibility, like most things with value, will take time and will need to start at home. Let me repeat this: responsibility starts at home for our children. If your children are too busy to have household chores, your family is probably over-scheduled. Take a good hard look at everyone's schedule. Are you on a parenting merry-go-round? If you are not taking the time to assign chores, you are not only cheating your kids from becoming independent and responsible, but you are also cheating yourself. Children need to have chores at home they are responsible for; but make sure they are capable of carrying out their duties. Assign chores by your children's ages, stages, and mental and physical capabilities. Begin with small, successful tasks. Give lots of praise. By assigning your children individual chores, responsibility is far from the only valid lesson that will be taught, and it is absolutely imperative for a growing preventive maintenance plan.

Think of delegating chores the way a CEO does in a business. If you will lead and model an example of how to get things done, your children will follow. This gives the Chief Executive Officer opportunities to obtain more free time for family members. Don't forget to include yourself in this plan. Make time for personal growth classes with friends or that exercise class you've been trying to get into. Exercising will give you a much-needed lift in motivation and other important health-related benefits. There will be more on this topic later. For now, keep in mind as your family team grows and changes, your guidelines will also. Be flexible and open to better solutions when re-evaluating and adjusting guidelines to provide the best plan for family success.

QUESTION: We are having problems teaching our children responsibility. Any suggestions?

A. Teaching responsibility for chores can be very time consuming. But believe me, it's worth it. Start training children with small successes as soon as they can begin to help put away their toys, somewhere around 14 months old. This may only seem like a baby step towards responsibility — and it is. But however small it may appear, it is still important for the future. Get into the right mindset about this whole endeavor and remember that things will not be perfect. First of all, you must lower your expectations and make it easier to accept the way smaller children get things done, especially if they are younger than 5. At around age 5, make up and discuss guidelines to be followed. More responsibility can be handed over and better results can be obtained as the children grow and mature. Allow children to fail. Again, this is worth repeating, let them make mistakes and learn valuable lessons. If you follow through on your part, a multitude of wisdom from logical consequences is lurking around each corner. One of the chores my kids are doing is folding clothes and putting them away. I have shown them several times how to fold T-shirts and explained to them the reasons why they are to be folded a certain way; i.e., so more would fit into a drawer. In the beginning I let them fold the shirts *their* way. Most young children and even some teens could care less about a wrinkled shirt, but the problem of diminished room in the drawer for other clothes quickly becomes frustrating. Voila! They learned a practical lesson: If shirts were folded neater and smaller, there would be more room in the drawer for other things, and the shirts will not be so wrinkled. My children are now refilling the dishes correctly in the dishwasher.

B. Don't correct your children's mistakes. After you're sure they know how to do something and they have proven this, stop showing them how to do it. Many times parents think it is easier to fix something themselves. Stop! Don't do it. Your children will become dependent on you for correcting their mistakes and finishing their jobs. This will end up as a disaster and explode down the road of parenting. Anger and resentment will begin to brew inside you. You may want to pack your bags and run off with the postal carrier.

Let children make and learn from their own mistakes. Otherwise, they will expect you to fix everything in the future. Of course, most children will try to test the waters at least some of the time. For example, they may have a tendency to give up on a new chore just to see how much you will do for them. Don't finish something that has been left undone unless negotiations are in acceptable terms between the two of you. It's not a problem for you to help out here and there, but do not redo things just because they are not up to your standards. Pick your battles wisely. There will be plenty of opportunities to pull out the "showstoppers" later (and it probably will not even be over chores). You are trying to teach independence and self-sufficiency. These are mainstays, which are essential for success in almost all areas of life. Teach and raise responsible kids; after all, you do not want them to come back home once they've left — except to visit.

C. Get to know your children as individuals. Put down the newspaper, book, or magazine you are holding. Turn off the TV, radio, tape, CD or computer. Sit down and focus on the person in front of you. That's right, go sit down. Tune in by really zeroing in on words and body language. It is of utmost importance to the family team that you find out about the individual personality traits of your members. Don't assume their likes and dislikes will be the same. They won't be! If you don't respect their individuality and accept it now, a dose of major grief will be handed over to you in the following years of parenting (especially in the teen years, if not before). Ask questions and be quiet and listen to the answers. I'm not suggesting you run a question and answer session to the third degree. If the situation is handled more like a friendly visit and your attention is genuine, this getting-to-know-you session will feel more like an interesting conversation. What is your body language saying? If you are rigid, the kids will be rigid as well. Don't drag this on and on. Stay tuned into the situation and spontaneity will help determine the time. Once again, ask open-ended questions. For example, ask what was something cool they did at school today? What was the least liked part of the day? You will not get a yes and no answer but maybe an honest and real response. In fact, the answer will hopefully move toward a conversation where the two of you can become better connected.

D. Spend time to find out what makes your kids successful. One of my children is very organized and quick to get things done and is quite successful in organizing closets, clothes, drawers and anything in view. Another is organized and quick to get things done only when he wants to. This is not to say once the chores are finally done, he has not achieved success. It's just a slower process with more probing before the task is completed. This doesn't mean, nor am I suggesting, giving all the hard jobs around the house to the child that works more efficiently. It is, however, pertinent information to consider if your family team's schedule suddenly becomes overwhelming for the day. If given the choice, the more efficient worker may choose to switch chores for the day. Allow for the time that it will take to teach a job done well. I promise (don't you hate it when people say, "I promise," but I am almost positive about the outcome) if you will take the time to teach your children responsibility now, there will be a significant reduction in the hassle department later on.

If you will look at teaching responsibility as a business plan (like a CEO in the business world would do), things may be easier to delegate. And for the record, please do not attempt to debate over the idea of *mere* moms being a CEO — because all moms have held the CEO title before anyone else! Think about it and let the title grow on you — and with you. You are the Chief Executive Officer of your household as you are Constantly Evaluating Others (as well as Options) for your family. The goal of a preventive maintenance plan will be easier to get started and easier to stay on track if it is successful. The follow-through will make everyone's life more enjoyable. The skills your children will learn will spill over into other areas such as homework and personal care. You are not only teaching and molding good citizens; you are also setting an example for your children's children because parenting styles are usually carried over for generations to come. Good habits learned early will last a lifetime and, of course, benefit society as a whole (not to mention building self-worth and pride in the child).

Motivating Kids for Positive Cooperation:

1. Let children know what you expect. Show and describe what it is you want them to do. Allow them to have choices on which chore to do first. As they get older, retrain and re-teach them for more responsibility. Don't lose your cool.

2. Be clear and firm but use a kind tone of voice. Have them repeat instructions back to you. Try to implement a preventive maintenance plan your family team understands. Let them help with rules and guidelines. If you need help, listen to business tapes, CDs or speeches. By simply changing some of the words, these same motivational techniques that train professionals in the business world can help train you for your home environment. I recommend a motivational book and tape series in Chapter 4 that has been used in many major corporations and seminars. Now moms can be encouraged by these same powerful thoughts and words of wisdom to be implemented in the home environment. Look in the index under "Leadership skills for moms."

3. Give your children a reason why. Explaining something should always include the reason why. It's OK to stop explaining if you've already said it many times. It may now be time for you to ask them to explain it to you. This will reinforce the instructions as well as make them have a better understanding of the subject. This guideline should apply to everyone: husbands, teenagers and smaller children.

4. With younger children use the phrase "As soon as." For example: "As soon as you put away your toys, maybe we can go to the park." Help them get started, or for children younger than 5, you may need to help with the whole task. As mentioned earlier, set them up for a mini success and they'll feel proud of themselves. Use the word "maybe" in as many sentences as possible instead of the phrase "we're going to." Try to avoid saying the word "promise." This will help later if for some reason the trip to the park, or whatever the situation may be, does not materialize.

5. If children make a mistake, don't say, "I told you so!" Actions speak louder than words. They know they've messed up. If they don't, take a step back and let the logical consequence take charge. If at all possible, don't let your children avoid the logical consequences learned through mistakes. The most valuable lessons are taught this way.

TIPS - (TUNED-IN PARENTS SHARING)

QUESTION: How can I make my children more responsible and respectful?

ANSWER: Present, support and facilitate the state of learning as a life-long process as well as an adventure. Don't look at it as a short-term goal. Teach life skills such as priority setting, time management, organization and resourcefulness through example and consistency. Affirm your child at every opportunity. Praise what is done right or well as opposed to "nagging or harping on" what is wrong. Value your child or children for who they are, not for what they do, produce, or achieve. "Worth" should never be performance based. - Sarah

ANSWER: I had a friend whose office was in her home. It was very important for her children to know when they could or could not come to her with matters. She wore a certain hat when she was working and did not want to be disturbed. After they learned to respect the situation, if they saw the hat on her head, they left her alone. She would take off the hat when she could give them time and attention. This worked out to be a very successful method. Although the kids are now grown and gone, she still puts on the hat when she needs to get down to business and begin her work. - Dottie

Mommy-CEO, adding wisdom: One of the best ways to help children become more responsible and respectful is through chores at home. There are certain things that need to be done before the children are allowed to play. Unfortunately, many times they wait until the last minute to do these and it cuts into their playtime. I am trying to show them how much easier it is on them (to say nothing of myself), and how much time is saved if they keep up with their duties on a regular basis. I am not a perfect parent by any stretch of the imagination, and some days, like many parents, I wish I wasn't one at all. It's much easier to just do the work myself! But taking the time to teach children respect for a job well done and to be responsible starts at home and will carry over into all areas of life.

QUESTION: Should parents pay for chores?

ANSWER: We do not pay our children for chores. It got to the point where they wanted to be paid for everything. Now, we simply spread out the chores among the children so the older ones do the harder chores and teach the younger ones as they get older. - S.

ANSWER: For routine chores, such as cleaning their rooms or doing dishes, we do not pay. We explain to them that everyday jobs are part of the responsibility of being in the family. For special jobs, like mowing the lawn or cleaning out the garage, we may agree to pay them a nominal amount. We tried an allowance with our oldest daughter, and chores weren't always done on time or not done well. I didn't like the power struggle it brought about. Now, we provide money for fun as needed, but it must be within reason. For something more extravagant, they have to work out their own plan to come up with the money. - Diane

ANSWER: Everyone gets a small amount of money for each room they clean. The amount increases if it is done before we ask for it to be cleaned. Credits are given for adding to the current list of chores without being asked. These credits are in addition to the money and can be used for free movie passes and other entertainment endeavors. - Sammy

Mommy-CEO, adding wisdom: We pay for chores at our house but require a healthy dose of cooperation. Set up guidelines your children understand. For example, if they are told to do a chore twice, the price is cut. If they have to be told a third time, no payment is given. They are paid on the same day each week and no advances are allowed. We have explained that each person is an important member of our family, and each person's contribution is important to have complete success. If their behavior is unacceptable for any reason, an amount is taken out of the payment. It's a lot of work to keep up with, but it can create a great sense of accomplishment for everyone.

QUESTION: My teenager seems to be slipping up on the rules of his curfew. What can I do?

ANSWER: I have three teenagers and so far this hasn't been too big of a problem. We have talked about the rules and have included them in the choices and consequences. If things aren't working out, it may be time to sit down with them and take another look at the rules. One thing that has seemed to help us is communication and the "have to" of follow-through. - C.

ANSWER: I use the same method that worked for my parents. Until we were 18, my brother, sister and I had a curfew of 11 p.m. At the age of 18, it moved to midnight. If we broke it, we were grounded one day for each minute we were late. I was only late twice: once for 11 days and once for 35 days. Of course, there were special occasions, like the prom, in which another curfew time was agreed on. This method works great with my 17-year-old son. I get a lot of ribbing and teasing about it because he is a boy. I'm sure he also gets teasing from his friends, but he never complains. I think it helps him to know that he can call when he's going to be late (which is very rare) and it will be OK. A successful curfew will work as long as the teen knows the reasons for the curfew are based on love by the parents. It also helps if he will understand that if he calls in for being late, he'll get to stay longer only because he's trusted. But if his late calls continue on a regular basis, then he's not respecting his parents or the curfew. If this happens, this is when you may be pushed into beginning to start counting the minutes. - P.

Mommy-CEO, adding wisdom: I remember quite well when our oldest son was a teenager and came in two hours late. The rules had already been set up and he had a significant part in helping to establish them. He couldn't go anywhere (including driving) for two weeks except to school. For each hour he was late, he would be grounded one week. He could have one friend over. At first, he and his friends thought this was simple and cool. They ate, played games, and watched TV. It became boring very quickly. While everyone else had plans, he had to stay home. Soon, even his best buddies were saying, "Sorry." The most embarrassing part was when I took him to school, practices, games, and (horrors of horrors) to the dentist. He asked if he could have any time off for "good behavior." There hadn't been any hassles, so I agreed to one day off.

Later, I heard him on the phone telling someone, "I'll meet you there." I said, "I meant you could have one day off by reducing the time by one day, not that you could go out tonight and be back on the grounding tomorrow."

Another person wrote in to tell parents to be aware that what we think is reasonable may not be reasonable to teens, especially if the concert begins and ends later than they thought. To try and remedy this challenge, teens should call home and clue in their parents to avoid trouble.

QUESTION: How do parents keep the Internet safe for their kids?

ANSWER: Our Internet provider allows certain accounts to be created with blocking devices appropriate for various age levels. Our children have been assigned screen names with the blocking device we felt matched their maturity level. Each screen name must have its own password typed in before it can be logged on. We have never told the children their passwords. They cannot log onto the Internet without our knowledge and approval. - Jeff

ANSWER: My children use the Internet for specific purposes. They can't just spend time surfing around or in chat rooms. This is enforced because the computer is password protected, so adult assistance is required to log on. With a computer-sophisticated kid you have to use a password in the "boot sequence," as opposed to using just a Windows password. It is very important that the computer is physically situated so that the monitor faces the center of the room and the door. When a child is on the computer, we make sure we're around and take look at the monitor. If they are caught poking into inappropriate locations, they won't be allowed back on for a long time. - C.

Mommy–CEO, adding wisdom: In our house, there's not much room for bargaining on this topic. Make sure your child's Internet safety is being monitored by someone or something for the best protection. If your Internet service doesn't offer any type of screening software, check out various packages at stores, on the Web, or ask other parents what works best for them. Don't forget to share concerns with your children and guidelines for not giving any personal information about themselves or any family member, such as name, address, phone number, school name, etc. When my kids come to me and say, "Mom, we're restricted from this site and we need to get information for a project at school," I type in my screen name and go to the site and stay there while they get what they need and log off.

QUESTION: Should I check my children's homework? And how's the best way to get them started each night?

ANSWER: With four children, we have to follow guidelines to make our household run as smoothly as possible. They are allowed to get a snack and take a little break, but it is short, and homework is top priority before any real playtime. By sticking with this rule, homework is usually completed by the time I need to start dinner. - Pam

ANSWER: Our household is very busy after school begins. Life with four kids can get wacky at times. The children get a snack and go play to unwind and take what I consider a much-needed break. We decide who gets help first with their homework based on the needs of each child. Or we may have to take schedules into consideration and be a little flexible. Sometimes, we may even have to wait until after dinner to begin or finish. - Sheri

ANSWER: It is important that parents share and discuss a child's homework. This helps the child to have a better understanding of the importance of school and the learning process. It will also give parents information about what's happening at school. The responsibility for the learning and actual work should be the child's and not the parent's. This is especially true as children get older. The homework can be checked to make sure it is complete, but not necessarily correct. - Julie

ANSWER: I have three kids in school — elementary through college. It is necessary to at least go over homework with the youngest. Extra time may need to be spent on a challenging subject. It's important to stress to them you are there not to push them to get an A but to guide them and reinforce what they are learning. By the time they get to middle school, you have hopefully given them a good foundation to make the transition to handle most of the responsibility on their own. - Kim

ANSWER: I am a single working parent and have children who range in age from 4 to 14 years old. Teaching children to be organized, self-reliant, resourceful, and consistent not only teaches them valuable life skills but can also be tremendous time savers. If your child says, "I don't get this," reply, "Just what is it you don't get?" What did you cover and talk about in class? Where else can you look for information? Children are terribly over-scheduled today and parents need to say "No" more often. Schoolwork needs to be the No. 1 priority. Parents confuse "helping" with browbeating and hovering. This presents a negative home environment and poor self-image to the child. If a parent does the homework, it will prevent the teacher from making a true assessment of the student's knowledge. Parents should offer tools and a quiet place to work along with guidance to enable a child to achieve. But let him do the work. - Sarah

Mommy–CEO, adding wisdom: You might want to answer a few questions before setting up rules. #1: Is your child a "super-achiever"? If he is, he's already had a very intense day and desperately needs a break. He may benefit from a five- to seven-minute break every 30 minutes or so. #2: Is he a "daydreamer"? Who knows what has been completed today? It's probably a good idea to let him have a snack and get right on with homework (it takes these kids longer to complete it). #3: Is he somewhere in between? Count your blessings and stick with a plan that is working. #4: Has he had a bad day? Diffuse the frustration by allowing some quiet time and then maybe talk about it. Sit down, look directly at him and really listen. #5: How's your outlook? Stay positive. With children up to second grade, it is definitely a good idea to sit down beside them and go over their schoolwork. From third to fifth grade, try to be around to at least guide them, but only if they ask. Try to encourage them to get in a habit of checking it over for themselves. Some mistakes can be found by slowly reading through it again. The best way to check math homework is by reworking the problems. From sixth grade on, it should be their total responsibility. Do what works best for your child in your own situation. Visit www.studyweb.com for plenty of help on homework.

QUESTION: My 14-year-old son is sneaking cigarettes. What should I do?

ANSWER: The ability of parents to influence their children declines over time. The influences of peers, TV, media, etc., take over. One area to control this is to take more responsibility for how much money you give them and what they spend it on. Without money, kids can't buy cigarettes, alcohol, drugs or guns. - Steven

ANSWER: Smoking often begins as a social activity of trying to fit into a new situation such as a group or school. Peer pressure is strong at this age and making drug education discussions now is a top priority. The American Cancer Society will send you tons of free information on the dangers of smoking. Have your teen take a look at it. - Elizabeth

ANSWER: We sat down with a calculator and methodically multiplied out the cost of a one-, two- and three-pack a day habit over a day, week, month and year. We even did it for 10 years, 20 years, 30 years, etc., and showed him how much it added up to — if he lived this long. He stopped! - J.

ANSWER: If you or someone else in your house is smoking, try to stop. If you set a good example, he may come around. If he is doing it for attention, let him know he's great without this unhealthy habit. - P.

ANSWER: I suggest you tell the kid to make payments on his own health insurance. If he wants to enjoy the trappings of adult behavior, then he can pay up for the appropriate responsibility. - S.

ANSWER: Let him smoke. If you try to stop him, it'll only get worse. Take him to the hospital and get an x-ray of his lungs now and go back in six months. It won't be a pretty picture. Ask the technician or even the doctor to show him x-rays of other long-time smokers' lungs. He'll be shocked! - T.

Mommy–CEO, adding wisdom: When I was in middle school, the American Heart and Lung Association held a fair on "polluted lungs." The pictures were blown up to emphasize each nook and cranny within the photo. We were all very much impressed by the black lungs. Call your teen's school and ask for a fair to be set up at your school. Pictures are worth a thousand words (and the parents won't be blamed for constant nagging).

QUESTION: Should parents pay for good grades?

ANSWER: No. Parents should not pay for good grades. Realistically speaking, we know that very little of the money paid for good grades actually gets into a college fund. More important, being paid in dollars creates an expectation of payment for any work done. Excessive pressure can be put on those children who may not ever be able to earn those A's and B's and in today's world, straight A's are not a guarantee to get the job in a specific career a college graduate desires. - Judy

ANSWER: Yes. We pay for grades because everyone else is doing it and it works for our family. Although we do not pay the regular $5 for each A, we do pay $4 for A's and $3 for B's. - T. B.

ANSWER: No. Don't pay for good grades directly. The child needs to set a goal and accomplish it. He needs to feel good about succeeding, and afterward the family can celebrate. Call their grandparents and brag, or go out for a special meal. Let the child pick the restaurant. - Jane

A professional shares: Parents absolutely should not pay for good grades. Concrete rewards have the tendency to lower the desire to achieve or compete. The parent's goal should be to develop intrinsic motivation, which comes from within the child. The internal motivation will serve the child longer and have a more profound effect than a concrete reward. Have high expectations, give support when needed, offer enrichment when possible and praise the specific accomplishment. - Dr. Hernandez

Mommy–CEO, adding wisdom: So far, we have not paid for good grades. We do, however, give a choice of a favorite restaurant or activity that would be a special family outing. We send photocopies of the report card to grandparents and friends and give big hugs and kisses. The blue honor-role ribbons given by the school are proudly displayed on the fridge and eventually are put into each child's "memory notebook" for safekeeping. At this time, we talk about a job well done and stress how good they must feel about themselves.

Mommy - CEO for Family Success on Golden Rule Three:

Teach children to do their jobs well. Parents need to take the time to teach children how to do a job well done. Responsibility begins at home. Offer choices and allow them to experience logical consequences that will teach and build character, self-esteem, cooperation, and independence — the list goes on. By taking the time to teach children responsibility — and implementing a preventive maintenance plan that your family team understands — life will be easier in many other areas. Values will be learned from a sense of accom-plishment and your family team  will appreciate and respect each other. Respect for family members, and even society as a whole, is missing in today's busy, over-scheduled children and parents.

PLEASE TEACH YOUR CHILDREN RESPONSIBILITY.

A Little Evaluation:

Making Time for Mommy

OK, OK, where was I? Oh yes, three tablespoons of butter and, "Someone please answer the phone. Honnneeyy, Keith, could you get the phone?" OK now, let's see, is the recipe calling for real butter? Or should I ... "Sorry, I can't come to the phone right now. Could you take a message?"

"Well, could you just make a decision about the final lawn application without me? I'm trying to get this last batch of cookies together before I run to pick up the girls from ballet and then dash to the grocery store!" As I gasp for a breath and try to rub my face out of frustration, cookie dough gets smeared onto my glasses. Great, JUST GREAT!

Holidays are wonderful, but after it's all said and done, is there any time left for me? Sure there is. But you have to grab it before it's gone. Believe me, girlfriend, you'd better schedule time for yourself NOW or there won't be any time left at all! As we all know, holiday schedules can bring an unhealthy dosage of guilty feelings. If you feel guilty, please do not! Your family needs to understand that moms need to have a "time out" too. Get your children to help with various chores and activities. Shoot for a goal, put together a plan and focus on getting all family members to join in so everyone can have a little extra time as well. If this is new for you, or if you've been doing it for a while, here are a few more tips that might help:

1. Tell your family when you will be gone on your time out and for what reason. Be very clear.

2. Unless someone is sick and there's no one else to watch the kids, don't listen to reasons why you shouldn't go. The chores and homework can wait, or your children can begin them without you.

3. If you don't take a time out, don't blame it on your family.

4. If you are sick, let them know you plan to make up your lost "alone time" at the next convenient opportunity.

5. Even though you love your family, strive to get out by yourself (especially during the holidays) if even for a little while.

6. Look around. Are there more chores around the house you could delegate to others? If so, do it. It is your role as the main caregiver to give your family members responsibility. This will take a load off of you.

7. Try not to take a pager or phone. Everything will be there when you get back. It's very tempting to try to finish one more task or to help someone with a chore before leaving. Don't do it. The kids need to be responsible for their own chores.

8. If you are exercising, listen to music while you're walking or running; don't only think about what needs to be done at work or home. While walking, many times I will use this time to pray about things that are of concern to me.

9. If you want to take along a friend, make sure they know ahead of time what you have planned and you both are in agreement.

10. Remind yourself often that while parenting and holidays are hectic, ask God for strength and guidance in getting things done and ask family members to pitch in as well.

Notes

_____

_____

_____

_____

_____

_____

_____

_____

_____

_____

_____

_____

_____

_____

_____

_____

_____

_____

_____

_____

_____

_____

4 | Golden Rule Number Four for Family Success:

Squash the overscheduling dilemma

"Slow down" is very easy to say, but very hard to do. Everyone's so busy these days. Parents seem to think the more activities they have their kids signed up for, the smarter and happier everyone will be. This is not true! In fact, more times than not the opposite will occur. Children will become so used to having an activity to fill their time, they won't know how to function without something scheduled for entertainment. Parents really go nuts in the summertime. The instant they hear "I'm bored," parents seem to panic. It seems as though children don't even have time to play with other children in an unrushed, UNSCHEDULED playtime. What has happened to family and personal time? Where is your preventive maintenance plan to keep everyone from burning out?

QUESTION: What is the best way of balancing being overscheduled?

A. Ask yourself these questions: Why is my family in such a hurry? Have I let my children sign up for too many activities? Am I signing them up to do these activities for them or for me? Am I signing them up because everyone else is doing it? Did we take other important things into consideration before allowing choices to be made? Did I personally make too many commitments that are causing me to become stressed out? Why do I "feel like screaming"?

Act on this situation now before it gets out of control. Get started today! Ask the children individually for a list of activities they would *like* to do. Make sure they know these are only their suggestions, and a detailed discussion will follow at a later date. For younger children, sit down and write out the list for them. Most children don't have a clue about what commitments will actually be required of them for certain activities. The bad news is, neither do the parents. Many parents do not even have the slightest idea of what school activities the child may want to enter into during the school year, which will only contribute to more chaos. Count these extracurricular school activities into the whole picture before making decisions regarding outside functions, clubs, contests, sports and lessons. As the CEO of your family team, it is your responsibility to find out information on the activity, including the number of practices and the locations. Gather the facts, review them and narrow the choices down to the two you can live with. (Two activities? Yes, two!) It can and should be done. If more parents and caregivers begin to say "No" more often, it'll catch on with other families.

B. Make a family chart out of poster board. With all of the new gadgets out today, you may be wondering why you should take the time to make a chart out of a poster board. Right? There are several reasons, with the first being this: to actually see things up close and together on a large piece of paper. Next, you can add the information into your computer calendar, palm holder or whatever you have handy to organize your schedule. Ask any CEO in the business world if charts are important. There's something about the magnitude of this huge family chart that really sinks in, believe me!

Make a family chart with goals for each quarter of the year; it will help immensely to see it all laid out in plain view. Give each person a column and expect everyone to compose an *acceptable* outcome at the bottom as a "total." The words used should describe the sum, goals or "total" of each person's column, such as, "Needs work," "OK," or "FLS" (Feel Like Screaming). If the total gets to the point of FLS, stop and start over. Include your children's school calendar along with any personal commitments other family team members want to make. Refer to these often while planning the chart. Write down goals for each family member. Try to limit activities to no more than one or two. Information on this chart should include practices and games, and how much time it takes to get to and from each one. Parents often overlook the time it takes to get from one location to another — it takes a big chunk of time out of the day and needs to be scheduled in. Call the coach or instructor and get specific details. This will give a more realistic picture. For example: If you have two children who participate in two activities each that require two weekly practices, that's eight practices for two kids! This doesn't even include the actual games or regular school projects like science fair, choir, band, art show, etc. Another slap in the face is that church and family time hasn't even been mentioned. As far as just plain old playtime with friends, this will soon appear on the extinct list!

What about taking personal time for yourself? And how about quality time with the other adult person in your house? You know, the one you sometimes pass in the hallway. Unfortunately, in today's world juggling schedules has become commonplace. Just don't over do it. Don't listen to what any celebrity or expert says if they claim it can be done without getting the entire family in a tizzy! It's not true, and actually is quite unhealthy. If you get the urge to FLS (feel-like-screaming) at any time while making this chart, STOP and review what's going on. Learn to say "No" to your friends and colleagues. Learn to say "No" to your kids. Practice saying "Yes" to your own personal time and to your spouse. (See FLS chart on page 81.)

C. Become educated on business leadership skills to become a winner. Tapes, CDs, television programs, books and seminars can help you run a smoother "home" workplace and squash the overscheduling dilemma. It will provide the ammunition you need for family success while incorporating time for yourself. There are several excellent leadership resources available. Many are located in the business section of a bookstore. Ask the sales clerk for help. He or she will know what's hot and leaving the shelves. I have read books and listened to many on tape, to speak nothing of attending seminars. The tape I liked the best is by award-winning author Dr. Denis Waitley, known best for "The Psychology of Winning." He was probably among the first to include moms and the family in his tapes. This gave me great respect for him and his work.

Family Team Schedule Chart   12 WEEKS

Goal: Church and family activity on Sunday

Family Rules: ① Homework before Playtime. ② Chores before Playtime ③ Bath before bedtime.

	Fido	Megan	Jake	Mom	Dad	Fluffy
	Obedience Class 2x wk 35 min. each 1 hr. 10 min	Soccer practice x2 each week 1 game ea. Sat. 1 make-up game	Soccer Practice x 2 each week 1 game ea. Sat. 1 make-up game	Exercise 1hr X 3 wk	Run 1 hr X 3 wk	Train to eat with fork like cats on TV. 2x wk 25 min. 50 min w/fork
	Practice 2x wk 30 min 1 hr		4 practices each wk 2 games each wk 2 make-up games wk	3 hrs. Drive to soccer Practices and back 15 min:2 hrs 4x2 kids	3 hrs Drive to soccer ½ time 1 hr 4 hrs	
			8 hrs wk	5 practices 4 games/20 8 hrs		
		Chores 3 hrs Church 2 hrs Family 3 hrs Basketball 1 hr (FOR FUN) Art fair 3 hrs	Chores 3 hrs Church 2 hrs Family 3 hrs Swim (FOR FUN) 1 hr Science fair 4 hrs	Chores 8 hrs Church 2 hrs Family 3 hrs Read 1 hr PT job 20 hrs	60 hr work sometimes more-65 Chores 4 hrs Church 2 hrs Family 3 hrs	
	Playtime 4 hrs.	Playtime 3 hrs Homework 2 hrs	Playtime 3 hrs Homework 2 hrs			
	**Okay :)	**Okay :)	**Okay :)	**Okay :)	:) *FLS RE-DO!	*FLS
	TOTAL 6hrs 10min	TOTAL 25 hrs	TOTAL 26 hrs	TOTAL 42 hrs :)	TOTAL 73 hrs	Total 1hr

*FLS = Feel Like Screaming :(

81

Just change the words to fit your own situation. Think of how to get yourself and your family motivated through his books and tapes to target a winning situation. (And yes, I wrote and asked him if I could recommend his work in my book.)

Sign up for business newsletters on the Internet and have them delivered to you. Make time to read material on a variety of business topics. To some of you this may sound odd. But it really does have a world of information for your home life. Learn to view your parenting career the same way many view other careers. The importance of learning the plans, goals and skills of a successful business can get you organized at home. These same organizational and motivational guidelines that are utilized in the office workplace can be implemented right into the home work place. Operate and run your family team like a CEO (Chief Executive Officer) would run a top-notch business organization. Getting organized and learning the tricks of the trade from business leaders can help to build a preventive maintenance plan for your family team that will last a lifetime. Only a few adjustments will be needed here and there for "good working order." There's no need for you to become a drill sergeant and drive your family (and yourself) nuts with every intricate detail. Just get the basic plan, let others know about it and change the terminology into words that best fit your own family situation. Add love and touch for the best recipe to achieve family success. (And don't knock it until you've tried it!)

D. Don't be in such a rush to get your babies and young children signed up for programs before the second (or possibly third) birthday. I'm not kidding!

There are many conflicting stories derived from "researchers" regarding early childhood academic education. Let your children enjoy being children. Tune in to your children's needs and make the best choice for your specific situation. If you choose a program and it doesn't work out, make a change. If you have the time and a little imagination, there's no need to go overboard with expensive toys and programs. There are tons of gadgets inside and outside the house to create a fun and educational environment right at home. Parents have a tendency to forget that everything is new and exciting to their children. There's no need for a formal learning environment with emphasis on academics. In these first two to three years, they're very busy learning to walk, speak and become coordinated, and trying to become an individual. They display a great zest for life and attempt to fulfill it daily. Motor skills and language abilities are growing in daily leaps, and depending on the child, they can be very happy and quick to learn rituals anywhere. Your community probably has a wide variety of activities for children of this age range. Check out the local libraries, community centers, zoos, parks and colleges for year-round activities. There may be many fun, stress-free programs. Begin with caution and proceed slowly. Remember that schedules can become out of hand very quickly. Think things through before signing up for too many organized playtimes. With all the hot new information out now on the developing brain of babies and young children, learning through playing will develop social skills and school readiness. Top priorities include talking, playing, singing, touching and reading with your little ones. This should begin as soon as possible after the birth of your baby. Or you could do what many people I know including myself have done: begin talking and singing to your baby while he or she is still in the womb. I know, I know, I said and thought the same thing: "Hellooo, we parents have been saying these very same things for years!" But hey — now the experts are finally coming around to agree about early baby language.

E. If you're thinking about leaving your children at home in the care of someone else, make sure you check references. It's best to try and find someone who has had experience with your children's age group and has taken some child developmental classes. Ask about educational classes they plan to take to stay current. Ask to see a CPR card and make sure it's up to date. Introduce the person to your children and watch them interact on several occasions. Invite the caregiver to visit at different times throughout the day for meals and to play. If the child is young, these visits should happen at bath time and bedtime. Give responsibilities during some of these visits and answer any questions as well as explain any rituals that may not be familiar. Get to know the person who will be taking care of your children.

If your children are in a childcare facility, make frequent unannounced visits during the week. In today's society, many childcare operations allow parents to "sneak a peek" online with their computers. Some even offer the opportunity to talk with your child over the Internet. To avoid miscommunication with the daycare, ask beforehand if the childcare operation has a policy that states a parent must notify the staff before entering via computer or the doorway. If they do, look elsewhere. You should have the right to "click" on at any time. Check out the playtime. Make sure there's plenty of time for children to just play and enjoy their surroundings without too much of a rigid schedule. Ask about the operation's teaching philosophy. Does everyone have to make art projects out of the same cutout patterns or can they use their individual creativity and imagination to come up with an idea? Are art supplies and age-appropriate toys on low shelves? Is an accredited program important to you? For a list of accredited schools in your area, contact the National Association of Education of Young Children at 800-424-2460 or visit their web site at www.naeyc.org for details. Find out the teacher/child ratio for your area and check on it. The most common are: one teacher to three infants, one teacher to five toddlers and 2-year-olds, one to ten 3-year-olds, and one to twelve 4- and 5-year-olds. When you are looking for childcare in your home, a childcare facility, someone else's home, or a parent's-day-out center, ASK PLENTY OF QUESTIONS BEFORE CHOOSING A PROGRAM FOR YOUR CHILD.

F. Never underestimate the power of prayer. Use prayer daily to help you with inner strength, wisdom and guidance for your family team. Whether we want to admit it or not, being a good salesperson, leader and teacher comes with the responsibility of having a family. Although I know it can sometimes be quite overwhelming and scary, we wear all these hats as parents. We wear many different hats throughout a marriage, during child rearing and in life in general. I could not do it alone. I'm not saying your children will always be perfect, or will you, but God can help us every day and in every way. Responsibility sets a solid foundation for individuals to come back to even if one should stray. Ask for help through prayer.

Motivating Kids for Positive Cooperation:

1. Turn a problem into a game. For example: "The first one to get all the dirty clothes into the laundry basket gets to choose breakfast." Keep special food on hand for choices to be exciting. This works with older kids as well.

2. Reduce extracurricular activities. It's driving everyone nuts! By using a family chart as a preventive maintenance plan, you can keep your team members, as well as yourself, in "good running order." Put your family team first and let God help you with the long haul and even everyday choices.

3. Never underestimate the power of prayer, and use it daily for guidance and inner strength. He knows what we need before we even ask.

4. Listen to leadership tapes and use them in your home workplace. They will help organize and motivate you. "The Psychology of Winning" series by Dr. Denis Waitley is my favorite. I've listened to many speakers, have read many books and have listened to all kinds of tapes; nothing has helped me more in my professional career as well as my family life than Dr. Waitley's material. You can take almost everything you hear and implement it into your family team plan.

5. Practice saying "No" to over scheduling activities, working and volunteering. It's not going to kill anyone and, in fact, it will help your family become healthier. Children need and want us to say this but may not know it. Children will always test the boundaries. As their caregivers and parents, we need to provide the guidelines.

TIPS (TUNED-IN PARENTS SHARING)

QUESTION: Any suggestions for taking time for yourself to help become a better parent? How can I get my own groove back?

ANSWER: I used to belong to a babysitting co-op and it was great to make new friends for the kids as well as for myself. Now that both children are in school, I find I can get that comradeship by meeting friends at some of the local bakeries and coffee shops. The coffee is great and the food is too. It's nice to have a place to meet friends and talk about children, school, church and community activities. It's also important to just be by myself sometimes, too. I think I'm a better parent because I take time out to go horseback riding on a regular basis. It gives me a sense of doing something for myself. - Jeanne

ANSWER: Take out time for yourself. Try to exercise at least three times a week. You will have more energy for your family and for yourself. - Pam

Mommy–CEO, adding wisdom: To get your groove back means different things to different people. It can reflect thoughts about schedules, habits, sex, body image and emotional stability. Many women are especially interested in this after giving birth. As you well know, our bodies are totally stretched out and way out of sync with what we would like them to be. This is perfectly normal; and even though your emotions are probably running high as well, things will get better if you work at it. YOU CANNOT BE EVERYTHING TO EVERYONE. My suggestion is to start saying no to people. Parenting is one of the most challenging careers you'll ever endure and I agree 100 percent with taking time out for yourself. Whether it's finding an organized support group, meeting at a coffee shop or doing something for yourself by yourself, make the time and do it. Take walks, read, exercise, ride horses or attend Bible study. It doesn't matter what you do as long as it is done in moderation and you are getting a small break from your role as a parent or caregiver. It will work wonders for your attitude, and your family will notice the difference. Eat well-balanced meals and get a support system going. Your husband will definitely notice the new, more energized you. And as far as the hubby goes, the lovemaking will surely follow.

NOTE: There is more on getting back your groove in Chapter 5.

QUESTION: How do I get my children to bed at night without repeating all the last-minute details over and over?

ANSWER: We use a bedtime ritual that was established before the children were born. I would sit at night and listen to classical music with the sound surrounding me while I read. After children were born, I put a CD player in their room and played the same music at bedtime. As they got older, I introduced different pieces of music that were all very soothing and low-key. There were usually no disturbances. The children have been able to identify with the music and consistency of the rituals because they have been exposed to it all along. - Sandra

ANSWER: With both parents in the household working and trying to juggle the kids' schedules, we have to be flexible. We are consistent most of the time with baths and stories until the spring and summer activities begin. Between practices and games, there is even a greater need for flexibility. Sometimes the kids do not get their bath until the morning. My oldest child got a clock radio from her grandmother for her birthday. The music wakes her and this has helped to get the mornings going smoothly with the things that couldn't be finished the night before. - Jana

Mommy–CEO, adding wisdom: It is hard to get little ones, as well as big ones, down at night in their beds for a final and last time. If you can find a regular bedtime routine that seems to work, then stick with it until you see a need to change. I used a "three times and you're out" rule with my kids. After story time and one last trip to the potty, I would allow them three more requests. As they got older, I would give rewards like a special breakfast or trip to the ice cream shop to encourage them to stay in their beds and to not call me back into their room. This worked well most of the time, but there's always going to be a night here or there when they just need an extra kiss and hug. If you give them a little extra time now, as they get older they should grow with self-confidence and go straight to sleep.

QUESTION: How can we not explode when our 9-year-old talks back?

ANSWER: When my children were this age and talked back, out came the pen and paper. We made them write 100 sentences in the exact words they said to me, which allowed it to sink in that it was unacceptable and not to be done again. We tried many things and this is the one thing they hated the most. It really worked for our family as well as our friends. - J.

ANSWER: Take everything out of the child's room except the bed and dresser. Each time he talks back, send him to his room. As he looks around, it will be empty with nothing to look at or do, and it will be a constant reminder of why he's in there. Don't make any exceptions. Let him know you want and deserve a sincere apology. - Patsy

Mommy–CEO, adding wisdom: Why all the backtalk? Stress, peer pressure, tiredness, daily physical and emotional changes, learning disabilities, diet (too much caffeine or sugar), too many movies, overscheduled, the list could go on forever. But whatever the reason, it's unacceptable and a hard uphill battle that leaves family members at wits end. In the 20 years I've worked with children and parents, it's plain to see that we view children as being weak and not as important because they are kids. The tendency to talk down, and sometimes with little respect, is overwhelming. Just as with any adult, children pick up on this right away and will try to compensate by getting attention any way they can. The first thing I try to get parents to look at is themselves. This is uncomfortable for most of us. Don't be threatened or become defensive; but while listening to him, do you hear yourself in some of his words? Have you been talking back to him? How's your tone of voice? If you feel you maintain a calm environment and tone of voice then, of course, it's time to dig deeper for the problem. Try and tape your evenings. Turn on a tape recorder while driving the car or preparing dinner and throughout the evening. Listen to the tape the next day. Most parents and kids are surprised at what triggers confrontations. Talk about what changes need to take place. Many times being overscheduled and running around without any downtime puts everyone on edge. Don't get pulled into an argument. Tell him it's not up for discussion until he calms down. Say nothing else. Don't shout or blame. Leave the room and talk about it later when everyone is calm. Get it under control now because soon the back talker will be a 15-year-old tyrant!

QUESTION: My 9-year-old daughter feels homesick every morning after I drop her off at day camp. How can I help her overcome this? Will it continue through the school year?

ANSWER: When our children go away, we send along a tiny photo album. They even take it along over "lock-in" sleepovers at our church or school. It contains several family pictures, including our dogs. During the school year, we switch to one that has a magnet on the back to hang inside their school lockers. - J. T.

Mommy–CEO, adding wisdom: Whether it's day camp or school, she may be trying to avoid someone or something. There are many reasons for kids this age to get this "homesick" feeling. Or she may be feeling too overscheduled. Ask her a few key questions: What's your favorite part of the day and why? I bet you can name at least five things you really enjoy about your teacher. What are they? What do you like to do with your friends? Don't react if she seems to get upset about a certain question.

I can't tell you how many times kids become stuck on a roller coaster of emotions just because we "overreact." They look to us for our opinions and reactions. Don't tell her she's being silly and there's nothing wrong.

Go in person to the facility and discuss your concerns with her teacher. Here are a few questions to present: Does she seem to get along with the teacher? When does she get homesick? Does it occur on days when a special activity happens? If so, how can she become better at this activity? Or are there too many activities scheduled? Are there any children who might be picking on her? How is the homesickness being handled? You may need to speak with the director or principal. If everyone is aware of the challenge, you may get quicker results.

In the future, for first-time day camp or school jitters, go to the school or camp together when very few others are around. The opportunity to visit and become familiar with her environment can make a child feel more comfortable.

QUESTION: Should my almost 10-year-old daughter be put on a diet?

ANSWER: How about a change of eating habits rather than a diet? The entire family could benefit from less soda pop, candy, cakes, cookies, chips, etc. Load up the meals with potatoes, brown rice, wheat bread, pasta and raw veggies. Use seasonings, salsa, and low-fat broths for taste. Fill up kids with nutritional foods and offer sugar-free or fat-free Jell-O and pudding. Now is the time to teach good eating habits and get the weight down, not when they are 16 or 18, when they are terribly ashamed of their appearance and are being teased. - Jill

ANSWER: The word "diet" should not be in her life! I have a sixth-grade girl and am trying to instill in her that she has to be comfortable with who she is. Part of that is keeping her body fit by eating right and exercising. I know there is a slight rocky road ahead for her and where the competition will be: Who will be thinner, more athletic, smarter or prettier? She will wonder where she fits in. This is why I stress that she has to be comfortable with herself. Sometimes I suggest taking a walk with me or playing a game of basketball in the driveway. I show her that you're never too old to keep moving. If we can teach our children a better way of life by not falling into the "snack attack" routine, a lesson of respecting your body and it respecting you should be accomplished. - Debbie

ANSWER: Children that are having a problem with their weight can develop a complex very easily. I would consult their pediatrician before adjusting their diet. I have seen many children who were excessively overweight slim down after puberty. Forcing a child into a strict diet can form unhealthy eating habits that will be carried into adulthood. I suggest looking at your family's eating habits and developing healthy diets for everyone. Cut out sweet snacks, chips, sodas and fast food. Provide your child with healthy snacks such as fruit and yogurt. My kids have always complained that I never buy sodas, cookies or candy to keep around the house. I occasionally let them have these when we are not at home. The key is to have everyone eating healthy and not to single out a child that is overweight - B.A.

ANSWER: No! It's unsafe before puberty to go on a diet designed to lose weight. I started crash dieting when I was 10. I was an anorexic by the age of 12. I was in therapy for my unhealthy body image until I was 19. I'm now 21 and I can't believe the damage I've done to myself. I'm four inches under my projected adult height, I developed asthma, my grades fell, and I ruined my chance of having children of my own. And I'm still unhappy with my body image. If this little girl wants to look like the women on TV or in the magazines, her mother needs to sit down and have a long talk with her about body images, air brushing for perfection and how advertisers aren't concerned about selling reality. If her daughter still wants to lose weight, she needs to sign up for summertime activities that'll keep her moving, eat healthy snacks and keep motivated for three months. The TV needs to be turned off and the fashion magazines need to be closed. - B.

ANSWER: I was "a little overweight" my whole life. My mom said, "It will go away dear." It didn't. If it is affecting your daughter's outlook, self-esteem, friendships and grades, put her on a doctor-appointed diet. - T.

Mommy–CEO, adding wisdom: If you eat healthy, your children will pick up on it. While you can't be around them 24 hours a day at the age of 10, you can try to alter what you bring home from the store. I'm betting that if you eat healthy and exercise, it will encourage them to do the same. Walking, running, basketball, baseball, soccer, swimming, biking, dancing, etc., are all great ways for kids to stay in shape. But how about those who don't like organized sports? Do some of these things with them "just for fun." When you go out for a walk, invite them along. If you use a lot of boxed snacks and desserts, add a cup of wheat flour to the recipe and switch applesauce for oil. After the third time you change the original recipe, try stepping up the nutrition by adding tiny pieces of carrots and/or zucchini to the snack. Even though the veggies are in small pieces, it makes the boxed snacks healthier. It works!

QUESTION: I travel for work. How can I keep a good parenting relationship going?

ANSWER: When the children were smaller, I would make up a calendar and mark the days that Dad would be gone and put a big "D" on the day of his expected return. Since their concept of time was limited, we would count "sleep days" and mark them off. We would usually get a phone call each night so he could tell them, "I will be back home in three 'sleep-days.'" This method not only helped them understand that they would see him after they had been to sleep three times, but it also gave them exposure to calendars and counting. On special occasions we tried to make "welcome-home" cards. - Missy

ANSWER: We make sure a couple of the children's favorite books are included in the suitcase. Daddy usually calls the kids after they have already taken their bath and are in pajamas. I usually talk with him first and then we put him on the speakerphone so everyone can hear his voice. He will read a couple of bedtime stories, sing along with a song, say a prayer with us and then tell us goodnight. By keeping our bedtime ritual as close as possible to the time we would normally share, we all feel much better. - Ellen

Mommy–CEO, adding wisdom: As the parent who stays home, it's important to keep your personal outlook positive. No one really enjoys when his or her spouse has to travel, and sometimes resentment builds up. The children may pick up on this and have mixed and confused feelings. When the traveling parent returns, make a big deal out of it and keep any frustrations and concerns undercover — to be discussed later and privately.

QUESTION: My 6-year-old stepson doesn't want to obey our rules on TV limits. How can I enforce these rules when he is visiting without all the guilt?

ANSWER: We created "TV Money." Each week we gave our son an allowance of TV Money that we made on our computer. We had $25, $50 and $100 denominations. An hour of TV time cost $100, a half-hour cost $50, and 15 minutes cost $25. Each time my son wanted to watch TV, he put that amount of TV Money in an envelope on my dresser. I didn't have to monitor him. He felt responsible for his time. He loved bragging that he got $1,000 a week for his allowance. - Mary

ANSWER: The key to survival is sticking by your guns. Look at kids' reasons, and let them know you are listening and are concerned. However, don't let them suck you into a guilt trip and win on those grounds. If you hear them out and believe their complaints are valid, let them know. If their complaints are not valid, just reassure yourself about the rules, and don't feel guilty for doing what is right in your house. Kids will respect you more when you stick by your guns. - A.B.

ANSWER: The programs my teenage stepdaughter is allowed to watch at home are unacceptable here because we have younger children who absolutely should not watch them. We asked her to be a good role model for the younger children. Since they idolize her every move, she agreed. This also made her feel important and very much a part of the family. - S.P.

Mommy–CEO, adding wisdom: Monitoring TV viewing is a challenge for most families. If children are in your home only a few days of each month or year, it can become a heated battle. It's best if parents on both sides can sit down and talk about it without the children around. Present the rules for your home in a way that does not make others feel as if they are the bad guys because they don't have the same rules. Maybe if you stress your belief that it is the best thing for the child, both parties might agree to implement the guidelines in both homes.

QUESTION: How can I keep my 7-year-old from crumbling over every little thing?

ANSWER: Some kids are just better at handling things than others. Structure and routine are the best way to handle crumbles. If you can set up her day so that she does the same thing at the same time, it will help her develop a sense of rhythm for her life. Let her aid in setting up and accomplishing those tasks even if it takes her twice as long as it would take you to do something. When things do go awry, maintain a good sense of humor. Show her that while things may not run as expected, it is easy to get them back on track. - D.C.

ANSWER: Whenever possible, give her plenty of advance warning of a change in routine. This will give her time to adjust. Be supportive and understanding that this isn't easy for her, but you have confidence that she will be able to handle it. Praise her when she does handle changes well. Recognize that she will likely always do best in a fairly predictable environment. Try to provide her with that structure while praising small steps toward flexibility. - Laura

Mommy–CEO, adding wisdom: Society sometimes places more dependency upon girls. If their world is shaken from unfamiliarity, they may make a fuss, whine or cry. This leads to intolerance of changes and usually gets worse as the child gets older. Her fears are probably very real and ingrained in her. Begin now by letting her handle small changes by herself. Ease into it slowly and give plenty of warning before a change takes place. Make sure she is not overscheduled, which will lead to being tired and frustrated. Set her up for small successes. For example: Give her a hug and tell her that from now on she will be responsible for putting up her bike and closing the garage door. Show her how to do it and then take the bike back outside. Go into the house, and when she comes in, say, "Good job!"

Mommy–CEO for Family Success on Golden Rule Four:

Slow down! Get off the merry-go-round and step off of the fast track of parenting! Set the tone for your family team. Don't sign up your children for a program just because everyone else is doing it! There's no need to put your BABIES AND YOUNG CHILDREN in a highly acclaimed early childhood academic program before the age of 2 (or possibly 3). Let your children enjoy being children. Take advantage of fun activities within your community or right at home.

As the CEO of your family team, develop the leadership role in yourself for your home workplace. Listen to tapes and read books on leadership skills. Use a family chart as a visible preventive maintenance plan. Transfer the information onto a calendar or into a computer system to get your family organized. This will allow you to measure your family team's goals. Never underestimate the power of prayer. God knows what you need before you ask and his wisdom controls our inner spirit and soul. Take time for your family and yourself. Whether your children are 2 or 18, they all need play time, fun time and time to just relax and chill out.

SLOW DOWN AND SQUASH THE OVER-SCHEDULING DILEMMA.

A Little Evaluation:

Follow the Yellow Brick Road When Choosing an Early Childhood Program

"Tommy, your barn is not the right color and your animals all look the same. All barns are red, not blue! Where did you get that blue crayon? Use the crayons I chose for you to color the animals in the picture and try to make your picture look more like mine."

I actually heard a preschool teacher say this. It happened to my son when he was 4. I hated it when he would come home with a piece of "art" that was perfect. Why? Because I knew he didn't do it. I knew blue was his favorite color and everything he colored was blue. I also knew nothing was supposed to be red, in his mind, except fire engines! I also could vividly imagine the teacher standing there with hands on hips, shaking her head with a big disapproving frown upon her face. I can also remember me asking, "Isn't it OK for them to pick out their own colors for the pictures?" I leaned over and took a closer look and found the barn to be rather small and the animals to be very skinny. Gee, I thought to myself, I don't know if even I could stay inside those lines. She looked at me like I'd just delivered the biggest insult of her career. She cocked one eyebrow and very sternly said, "Young lady, I've been teaching preschool for 20 years. I think I know what's right!" I felt like hiding under the table. I felt like running away. I felt like crying, and so I did! As I grabbed a Kleenex, left the room, got into my car and drove away, I thought to myself, "What have I done?" This was only his second day of school and I've already started a fire that might not ever go out. I've disputed the word of the "Great and Powerful Oz" and now my child will suffer! Well, what is the big deal about having a blue barn? What's wrong with having all the animals the same color?

What's wrong with this picture is not the fault of my little boy. What's wrong is a teacher who obviously doesn't know a whole heck of a lot about 4-year-olds, except how to get them to do things exactly as she wants. I don't care if she's been teaching 20 years. If I feel this bad, how does he feel? Doesn't she realize what could happen to a child's self-esteem if he heard similar remarks on various projects over and over for weeks upon end? Would she ever notice if he became withdrawn and quiet? Would he ever trust his ability to choose? Would he take a chance to display a creative bone in his body on anything ever again? Did he feel like running away or hiding? Did he want to cry? Was I overreacting? I could wait and see. It wouldn't be the end of the world if we just waited a few more weeks. As I turned my car back toward the school and checked my son out of the class, I felt like I had claimed my ruby red slippers — or blue or yellow or whatever color I wanted them to be.

For each one of you struggling with the color of your slippers and trying to make a decision on choosing the right early childhood education program (whether it be preschool, nursery school, a childcare facility or a parent's-day-out program) for your precious little one, go and visit. Stop, look and listen. Here are a few things you may want to consider: Find out who your child's teacher would be and ask about her background. A degree or experience is great, but like a lot of things in life, it doesn't make for a perfect situation in teaching or in any other profession. What developmental classes has the teacher taken recently, or how is she keeping tuned in to "current" changes? Does she seem to have an answer for everything or is she asking questions about your child? Is she listening to the answers? How many children are in the room? How's the interaction between her and the students? Does she have a smile on her face? Do the children smile and want to hug her? Does she let them? Does she hug back? Check to see if there are art projects hanging about. Do they reflect the encouragement of individual creativity? Are the toys on low shelves? Are they age-appropriate? Do they have "dress-up" play stations with hats and outerwear for both girls and boys? Is there an inside and outside play area? Ask to see their policy manual on holidays, sick days, snacks, etc. Do they offer the things you are interested in getting your child to experience and to learn about?

If you'd like your child to learn more through play as opposed to academics, find out about their curriculum. What is their teaching philosophy? Is an accredited program important to you? This is not to say that if the ones you like best are not accredited they may not be as good or as highly recommended as the others.

Now, find out what is important to you, make out your list of questions, set out on the yellow brick road of guidelines given to you here, and go ask those questions. (Of course, you may have to leave Toto at home!)

Notes

_____

_____

_____

_____

_____

_____

_____

_____

_____

_____

_____

_____

_____

_____

_____

_____

_____

_____

_____

_____

5 | Golden Rule Number Five for Family Success:

Don't forget the little things that count.

Through all the rushing around and moving in every possible direction, SOMETIMES WE OVERLOOK THE LITTLE THINGS. They are small and seem to be insignificant. However, little things can sometimes be the most important ingredients for family success. They are just as important to each individual as they are to the backbone of the family team and your preventive maintenance plan. If you think a hug or a smile can't or doesn't make a difference, think again. It might make the recipient of the small but important gesture have a whole different kind of day than what they thought was in store for them.

QUESTION: What's the best way to get through parenting without losing our minds?

A. Parenting is tough, but don't forget humor. Try not to take everything so seriously. A little humor can go a long way in many situations. I use it on a daily basis. Laughter is truly some of the very best medicine. Children enjoy seeing their parents/caregivers act a little wacky. I use it often to get my children, as well as others, going on a chore or project. For example, if you have a child who sticks everything under his bed and everything you've done so far to correct this problem has failed, try this: After the child has announced he has finished cleaning his room, ask him to meet you there in five minutes. Get down on your knees and hold your breath and take a long hard look under the bed. Without yelling or screaming (even though I know you would like to), begin to remove the "things" underneath. Make silly comments about seeing things for the first time. Have two socks talk to each other. Put one on each hand and say, "Oh, so there you are, Sam. I thought you were lost forever." Sam answers, "No, I've been within a few inches of you this whole time. I just had a checkerboard squashing me!" Before you know it, your child will be joining in and pulling out things, too. My husband, who says I never give him credit for any of our "silly" and creative games, came up with another fun idea that the kids enjoy. To get them to help out with the boring job of picking up pinecones in the yard, he brings out a huge trashcan and creates a competition called "Who can make the most baskets?" He's a sports nut and quite often gets the kids started on their chores by making up a family sporting event. He even has a saying that goes along with many of the "projects." He will ask, "Whose a team?" and the kids will answer, "We're a team!" And of course the kids love this and enthusiastically say it back for the next few minutes. They not only have fun but it also gets chores done in a family "project" as a team.

B. Give a hug and say, "I love you!" It doesn't matter if your children are babies or if they are seniors in high school — give them a hug. If you have older kids and haven't done it lately, try it. They need it and so do you. At this point in your relationship with your children, you may think it's necessary to start off with a pat on the back and eventually graduate to a hug. That's OK. In fact, a smile is kind of a hug, but try to work on that physical contact. This lets your children know they are important members and players in the family team. Say "I love you" more often and put feeling into it. How often do we say those words out of habit? It's kind of like hearing "Have a good day." After a while, as with many things, it will get tuned out. Beginning today, think about it when you say those three little words. Emphasize your feelings with a hug. Pray for guidance with your family and for your own leadership role.

C. Never stop dating your spouse. Before my husband and I got married, a marriage counselor told us to never stop dating. Make time to have a "date" at least twice a month. Amazingly enough, many couples I talk with just don't take the time to be alone. There's no need for your evening to be expensive every time. Choose and call ahead for an early reservation at a restaurant. Many restaurants offer early-bird specials for people to take advantage of. Go to an early movie. In many cases, this is when the best prices are offered. Or eat at home and go for dessert after the movie. If weather permits, pack a dinner and go to a park. When is the last time you and your spouse had a picnic alone together, without kids? For many of us, we have a tendency to get into a daily rut. Everything is done out of habit. Break the habit and get into a whole new situation. Sometimes doing something you used to enjoy doing together, but haven't since the kids arrived, may be just what you need to rekindle that earlier flame. Farm the children out, stay home and take the old records off the shelf (OK, OK, a tape or CD), and dance the night away. Check out videos and music from the library. Practice and learn new dances together, laugh, act silly and have fun! Play a variety of music. Make up some other fun activities. It really does make for better parenting. It's time spent just for the two of you to get caught up on things and enjoy each other's company without children around. See important daddy tips at end of this chapter!

D. Spend time with each child separately. Plan a "special time" with your children as individuals. For example: Mom takes out the 10-year-old for a burger and a movie alone. Dad takes out the 8-year-old for a taco and a trip to the local bookstore. Keep a record of who takes which child out last and then switch. Away from all the daily hustle and bustle, you'll be pleasantly surprised at how nice this can be. It's absolutely mind-boggling to find out how much of a delight a child can really be when you're alone together. Kids love it, too. They enjoy the special attention and the opportunity to have the spotlight "just on them." It works wonders for their disposition. Kids change and so do their ideas. This is the perfect opportunity to listen to their viewpoints and ideas on various topics. You will find out many things that you thought you already knew. Of course, if you miss sibling rivalry and glow of being a referee, you can always omit this suggestion.

E. Make time to do things as a family. Try to do things as a family at least every other week. When was the last time you and the whole family went on a walk in the park? If you don't have the time to follow some of these suggestions, your family is overscheduled and may be on a path to an unhealthy lifestyle. Things done for pleasure as a family don't have to be expensive. In fact, money can buy only material things that don't hold water when it is compared to quality family time. Take a bike ride, plant flowers, plant a vegetable garden, play basketball, have a tea party, pray together, read together, play a computer game or better yet, play a card or board game. Put on a play and get those creative juices flowing. Sing and dance together. Try to develop family traditions throughout the year. Set a goal to make holidays and special occasions simple and to enjoy each other. Plan ahead and try to make homemade gifts and cards for family and friends. With busy schedules in this day and time, the discipline and effort put into these presents will be quite impressive and very much appreciated. If you have to begin making Christmas gifts in July to be ready in December, schedule it into your family plans and make it part of your goals in the beginning of the year. It shows your children that the little things in life are worth preserving. Make memories that will last forever. Having fun together is a major contribution to a secure and successful preventive maintenance plan, but everything will not and does not end up being fun. For example, volunteering a few hours each month at a home for disadvantage children, an animal shelter, a handicapped children hospital or a senior citizen facility may not be what kids think of as being fun, but your display of empathy and kindness speaks volumes to your children in important ways. By offering your time to others, you are setting the stage for a lifetime of learning for your children to model. They need to know how important giving of one's self can be in helping to make a difference in the world. You can find balance in your life by setting goals and doing things in moderation. Grow your spirit with God and strengthen your relationship with Him.

Motivating Kids for Positive Cooperation:

1. Stress cooperation. Explain to everyone the concept of the family team and how important each member is to the team as a whole. If a child is too young to grasp the concept, make her feel important and appreciated in other ways. Clap and smile when she cooperates and say, "Good job — way to go!"

2. Use humor whenever you can. Get creative! With younger children (who are already sometimes too silly for words), if things get out of hand, keep it short and simple. Your tone of voice can indicate when "fun time" is over. Change the subject and move on to something else.

3. Give hugs and say, "I love you." You need this as much as they do. Do it with feeling! For older kids, give a hug — they will be surprised and will probably really like the attention. Hugs are a little freebie but packed with an enormous punch. Do you have kids in middle or high school? Who cares? They need hugs, too.

4. Make time for a family activity at least every other week. Enjoy each other and let the children take turns picking an activity. Taking kids here and there to a practice or game is not what I'm talking about here. Quality activities mean slowing down and doing fun but important things together.

5. Learn about your children's individual personalities. Spend special time with each child. It's kind of like a date, but with your kid. The one-on-one time is invaluable in getting kids to open up in conservation.

TIPS (TUNED-IN PARENTS SHARING)

QUESTION: How do other parents curtail tattling?

ANSWER: Due to an illness, I had to stay in bed almost an entire summer. Whenever one of my four children tattled on another (or whenever there was a ruckus outdoors), I called out loudly: "Attention, everyone front and center!" All four kids had to come in from playing and line up at the foot of my bed. Then the initial complainer stated his case, and thereafter each child was obliged to tell the story from his or her point of view. No one was allowed to voice the slightest objection while another was talking. After that process was done, each child had to state how he or she could have acted to keep the problem from happening in the first place. This only had to happen about four times. All four agreed it was so boring that they would make a peace agreement among themselves outdoors so they wouldn't have to go through it again. - Jo

ANSWER: I urge parents to be discerning in what they label "tattling." When a child reveals a violation of rules (set by adults for the welfare of children) only to be reprimanded and criticized, the message sent is that the crime of tattling is somehow worse than the original offense. - Lois

ANSWER: We made a distinction with our three girls between "telling" and "tattling." We feel if some things are left unreported to the adult in charge, it could lead to harm to one or more persons, property or programs (of benefit to all parties). Our basic teaching was this: If it's a rule that applies to everyone's good, one should tell the adult in charge if it is broken. Only in an "emergency" should one kid intervene to prevent another's actions. An example: A smaller child wandering out into the street is an "emergency" and should be brought back to the yard. But two kids fighting on the school playground is serious and an adult should be notified right away without intervention. We defined "tattling" as telling on someone else mainly to get that other person into trouble. Tattling was easily identified by asking the child to think first of what harm would come to him or anyone else if he ignored the other kid's words or actions. - Sharon

Mommy–CEO, adding wisdom: Here are a few other guidelines that might help:

If there's no hitting or dirty words, don't intervene automatically. Children have to learn to work out their own confrontations. Make sure the rules at school and at home are similar. If a child is tattling to get the other one in trouble, look at the child and calmly state: "I'm sorry, but I can't help. You need to work it out between yourselves." For children under the age of 7, many parents give an example of what could be agreed on, but then let the kids decide on the final compromise.

QUESTION: How can I exercise without feeling guilty about taking time away from my family?

ANSWER: While the kids stayed home with their dad, sometimes I felt guilty while swimming at a local health club. But then I realized it kept me sane for the many parenting challenges I faced alone while my husband traveled during the week. Get into something you like and try to stick with it. Your whole family will benefit from your wellness. - Sheryl S.

ANSWER: My first suggestion is stop feeling guilty! All you need is 30 minutes a day. I do try to include my 9-month-old son when possible by taking him with me when I jog or walk. He really enjoys the ride. When riding the stationary bike, I bring him into the room with me along with his favorite toys. He plays while I exercise. Anything that requires more concentration, like exercise videotapes, I use when he's taking a nap or having quiet time in his room. - J.B.

ANSWER: Exercising to stay healthy to raise your family should not make anyone feel guilty, as long as you don't overdo it. There are some people who get such a rush out of exercising they neglect their family. You can make your whole family healthier by exercising as a group. Make it fun. While doing sit-ups, have your children sit on your feet and help you count. Then you hold their feet. If children are too little to keep up on a walk, use a three-wheel exercise stroller. Use your imagination to exercise with your children. You could also have someone watch your children while you jog or walk, then switch off. - Kate

Mommy–CEO, adding wisdom: Your life will change drastically after children arrive on the scene. Please take time out for yourself. So many moms today feel overworked, underpaid, not loveable and totally unacceptable to others and themselves. For example, one time several weeks before a speaking engagement, I asked several major companies and school districts in the area to offer a topic sheet to employees who could check off what they were interested in hearing me talk about. There were several choices. The two choices that received the most votes were how to stop screaming at the kids and become a better tuned-in parent, and how to take time for yourself without feeling guilty. Although the companies employed both genders, only three men sent back the form while over 4,000 women replied. When it came to the part about feeling guilty, many women wrote notes on the form and some even took the time to send in personal letters. Their letters and notes took on the same tone and were truly shouting the same messages. It was loud and clear that they were consumed with guilt about working. They told stories how they were lost as to how to be a good parent and still take time for themselves (getting their groove back) without feeling guilty! They couldn't find balance no matter how hard they had tried. To tell you the truth, it bothered me so much, I called some of the companies and suggested programs to be put into place immediately to help meet the frustrations of their female employees. I even offered to come and talk with the women in a "lunch bunch" session but ended up moving out of the area and never got a chance to follow up.

But as you can imagine, many moms have this very same feeling. It doesn't matter if we're working in or out of our homes. Sometimes we all feel strapped or trapped. Why do we have this image of "doing it all"? The media tell us to find a balance in our life. They show us celebrities and high-power people in the spotlight that seems to be doing it all. But I often wonder if women who work outside the home or even inside the home can truly accomplish this without slowing down and focusing on their spirit. Personally, I think they cannot. When I'm consumed with fears and questions, as for everything else, I go to God in prayer. You know, he may not answer us right away and it sure as heck may not even be the answer we're looking for, but his power and words in the Bible can only help. Read your Bible, join a support group, eat better and exercise for a healthy, better you and many other challenges will fall into place. Grow your spirit with the Lord. Everyone will notice and your husband will be just as proud of you as you are of yourself. Don't ever forget this!

When you exercise, let your kids see you in action and place a star on the chart each time you exercise. Invite them along if you're going outdoors. They may slow you down, but that's OK for a couple of days a week. Add their name to the chart and put stars up by the dates they exercise with you. Turn on the radio or play a favorite piece of music and dance by yourself or with the kids. It's a total body workout, it's fun and they love it.

QUESTION: How can I get my kids to pick up dirty clothes from their bedroom floor?

ANSWER: Get everyone together and make the announcement that from this day forward, you will no longer be responsible for picking up dirty laundry and will only wash what is in the basket. Four of our five children cooperated right away, but "Mr. Holdout" waited a little too late, which was apparent to him all of a sudden when he had no clean underwear. "What do I do now?" he asked, and I calmly replied, "Wear what is available or wash out a pair!" It is important to stick with your rules. - Pauline

ANSWER: I found that handing over the responsibility of my children's rooms to them made a big difference. Let them decorate and arrange their space the way they want. It builds self-confidence and respect in them. It may take a few reminders and a helping hand from time to time (only for the smaller ones) but eventually, when there are no clean clothes or they can't find something they need, they'll get tired of the mess and clean it up. - Cheryl

Mommy-CEO, adding wisdom: This can be a power struggle between children and their parents. Having them become responsible for their own laundry works wonders. If this is a challenge for a child younger than 12 who thinks he's 22, let him experience running out of clothes. For children 12 or older, teach them how to do their own laundry. This will take time and effort on your part but will be well worth it. Get creative! Take them to the store and let them pick out their own detergent and fabric softener. It may seem trivial, but it counts in a big way to them. You also are making a very significant statement: "You are now responsible for your own clothes."

QUESTION: When my kids come back from visiting their father, should I listen to their complaints about his girlfriend?

ANSWER: When my ex-husband and I were first separated, I was advised not to ask any questions when my children came back from seeing him. That was bad advice. My daughter thought I didn't care about her and withdrew from me and everyone else. I did not want to be obtrusive in her and her brother's visits with their dad — but I did want them to know I cared. I started telling them about my weekend and listening to them talk about theirs. It was easy to help them talk without being obtrusive. My children and I have open communication now. - Kate

ANSWER: Listen to your children because it may be a legitimate concern — hitting, drugs or any assortment of things that could be harmful to them. If this is the case, talk to your ex. If you think the children just don't like the individual, have them sit down with their father to explain their concerns. Never brush off a child who wants to talk. The child's concerns may or may not be legitimate, but talking will help work out the problems. - T.

Mommy–CEO, adding wisdom: Handling this situation is going to depend on many things: the age of the children, the relationship between the father and mother, and the relationship between the father and his girlfriend. Here are some tips:

Make sure the children know both parents still love them. Let children know the divorce is between Mom and Dad and is not their fault. Children automatically blame themselves for a divorce. They think if they had been smarter, quieter or nicer, Mom and Dad still would be together. Listen to your children's complaints but don't jump to conclusions. Try to not ask personal questions about the other parent's life. Unless you see physical injuries or inappropriate emotional display, keep your ears open and your mouth shut. There's a wide range of emotional swings during a divorce, and children can feel guilty if they have a good time with the opposite parent. Ask the children about their visit later as opposed to sooner. This will give them a chance to unwind and might even provide an opportunity for them to say, "I'd like to talk about Dad's girlfriend now." Just listen and try to stay calm. Give them a hug while keeping your tone of voice low and reassuring when you do speak. Call your ex-spouse and set up a time to meet. Try to not make an emotional phone call. For immediate relief, call a friend, pastor or your own parents. By talking with others, you may come up with an idea on how to better handle the situation.

QUESTION: I have a very wiggly toddler who makes it almost impossible to change his diaper. Any suggestions on how to get him to be still during the process?

ANSWER: I know just how you feel. My 19-month-old never wants to stay still while I change his diaper. Something that has worked for us is changing him in the bathroom. It's the warmest room in the house, and I have an Elmo's Light & See propped up next to the tub. It's situated so that it doesn't move when my toddler pushes the buttons. This way he can play while I change his diaper. He loves the toy because it has lights and motion. - Debbie

ANSWER: When my second child turned into a wiggle worm while we tried to change his diaper, I implemented a plan: I changed him on the floor. This way he couldn't fall off the changing table. I had all the supplies ready. I had to get the diaper changed in a matter of minutes. If he tried to roll over, I gently

placed the tips of my bare feet, no shoes, on his shoulders with my heels on the floor. He thought this was fun and it worked for us as a game. Be quick but gentle, and let them sit up as soon as possible.
- Rebecca

ANSWER: Try giving the toddler a toy that he enjoys and will keep both his hands occupied. You might also talk to him about why he needs his diaper changed. For example: "Mommy has to change your diaper so you will not get a rash and have a boo-boo. After I change your diaper, we can go play!" You can even explain what it is: you're changing a wet diaper or bowel movement. This will help later in potty training.
- Dorthea

Mommy–CEO, adding wisdom: OK, go ahead and laugh, but here's what worked best with my family: I would always sing a song about an invisible dog. They loved it! I made anything up and barked. I would say, "Shh, be still. I hear a puppy dog barking. Listen." I then barked, sometimes loud and sometimes soft with eyes as wide as they'd go. I'd say, "Oh, let's hurry up so we can look out the window and see if we can see the pretty puppy dog!" We'd hurry and finish and run from one window to the other. Of course, we were both laughing. It worked every time. Honest. It sounds far-fetched, but who cares as long as they liked it and we had fun? Just call me goofy, but it's worth a shot.

QUESTION: I am three months pregnant. Our first baby died of SIDS and we are scared. What have other parents done in this situation?

ANSWER: We lost our first baby from SIDS, and eight months later we were excited and scared about being pregnant again. Our doctor put our next child on a monitor and ran a test while he was still in the hospital to monitor his breathing and heart rate. We took the monitor home with us as a security measure. After we got the OK, we took off the monitor. Each one of our next three babies was tested before they left the hospital and monitors were sent home. It's still a scary situation, but I would have been a nervous wreck without the monitors. - Karen

ANSWER: Try and line up the proper support so that you can successfully breastfeed your baby. Studies have recently shown that there are fewer incidences of SIDS among breastfed babies, most likely due to the decreased allergies and respiratory infections as well as the other health benefits. Also know that it is OK to have the baby's crib or bassinet in your room next to your bed so you can check the baby often. Having them sleep near you even helps regulate their breathing since they tune in to your natural sleeping rhythms. You will also be right there to notice any irregularities, which will be reassuring. - Karen

Mommy–CEO, adding wisdom: Many things factor into providing a safe environment for newborns. It is now suggested that newborns be laid on their back to sleep, and never give baby a binky with a string attached to it or any other item with a string. This will hopefully prevent strangulation. Hair spray, paint, aerosol sprays, cigarette and cigar smoke, and yes, even pet hairs are all among the priorities at the top of the concern list. Keep fuzzy stuffed animals, toys, pillows, puffy bumper pads and cats out of the crib. This stuff may sound small and insignificant, but truth is known, it adds up. For moms who nurse: Listen to your doctor about what you are putting into your body, which might affect the baby. Think healthy and read all labels. Many of these things are more damaging to babies prone to asthma and allergies than to others. Unfortunately, we usually don't know what the baby is allergic to, or even if they have asthma, until they're older. For safety's sake, don't risk it.

QUESTION: What skills do kids need to have before starting kindergarten?

ANSWER: Don't worry about specific skills in preparing your child for kindergarten. Read to your child every day from the day you come home from the hospital. I taught school for 25 years and know there is nothing you can do that can be more helpful. - Ann

ANSWER: The most important skills that a child needs is to be able to listen, follow directions and speak. It is also very important that he learns to work with others. Begin with the simple things, and the child will pick up many skills necessary for kindergarten. I read with my son and emphasize the different sounds and pictures in the books. Let the child be actively involved by allowing him to turn a page or point to a picture. Ask questions while reading. This allows the child's mind to formulate a response and make a connection between what you are reading and the question. - F.

Mommy–CEO, adding wisdom: Reading, talking, asking questions and getting a child involved in everything possible will provide a healthy boost to readiness for kindergarten and life in general. By now, most kindergartners know the alphabet, and many can write the letters. I'm still a firm believer in the magnet alphabet letters placed on the refrigerator. They can see them several times a day and play with them. They also teach colors and enhance fine motor skills by taking them off and on the fridge. This helps build hand-eye coordination and balancing skills, which are a must for correctly holding a pencil. Working puzzles can also help develop the strength and steadiness to use scissors (which can be very frustrating for a kindergartener if he feels behind the others in cutting). By the way, these fine motor skills in the fingers often develop a little later in boys, or those who use their left hand. But by all means, if your child prefers his left hand to the right, let him do it his way. Teach your child how to answer questions about personal information. By now he should know his complete name and how to spell it, phone number, city, state, house number and street name. Remember, I didn't say write it, only know it. So, no panicking, moms and dads!

QUESTION: How can I begin simple traditions with my children at home?

ANSWER: I am a single working father, and my time with my daughter is precious. With our hectic schedules it seems as if she is growing up overnight right in front of my eyes. We try to plan something special at least once a week. It may not be elaborate or expensive, but whatever we do, we do it together. This is a time of fun and communication between us. Going out to eat and to a movie is great, but we have just as much fun eating and watching a movie at home. We don't talk about pressures at work or school unless she brings them up. Almost every Friday night ends up being our "fun night" with each other. - Dan

ANSWER: I have two daughters and every week we have a "girl's night out." My husband plays cards with his friends, and we girls get together and have fun. Working in a salon has taught me how positive a little extra personal attention makes my customers feel. I decided my daughters would enjoy this. I wash, condition, and fix their hair. The hands and nails are next. Fingers and cuticles are massaged with special creams. Then come facials — and pedicures, which relax everyone. This weekend makeover takes several hours — plenty of time for us to get to know each other and talk about many things. We've been doing it now for a few years and I know of no better way to build a lasting relationship while opening up the line of communication. It's getting nicer as the time passes because now I'm getting back what I've put into it; they're actually getting good at pampering me!
- Terrilyn

Mommy–CEO, adding wisdom: Actions do speak louder than words. Children need to learn the value of enjoying simple things. We parents feed into their expectations. If we are rushing them from here to there and giving in to their every whim, what will they need and expect in years to come? Expensive clothes, toys, games, trips, etc., will cause their "I want" lists to become excessively long and their self-centeredness to multiply. Before you know it, they'll be grown and gone and you'll wish you had made the time to have really gotten to know them. Sit down and play a board game (remember those?), play cards or take a walk. The lines of communication may open up. And who knows? They may like it so much they'll ask to do it again.

QUESTION: My daughter has a learning disorder. Should we tell our other children, or should we treat her the same?

ANSWER: Yes, tell your other children. This will give them the opportunity to understand that your daughter learns differently and that she will have different needs than they have. I don't think you'll be able to treat your daughter exactly the same as you treat your children who don't have a learning disorder. For example, she may require extra time to do tasks, or you may have to explain to her several times how to do things. If your other children understand that your daughter has a real need for these things, they may be less resentful of the extra attention she will be getting and may even come up with their own ways of helping her. -Mary

ANSWER: When we couldn't take the behavior any longer, we took my son to a psychological center recommended by the school. He had ADD. We put him on Ritalin, and it calmed him down so he could concentrate better. By the time he reached puberty, we took him off it. His homework had to be done in five- to 10-minute spurts with plenty of breaks. We told our other children and other adults, but we tried not to treat him differently. We did not give him a chance to use this as an excuse. What I did was make my presence known at the school. I volunteered and tried to help in areas where I could get to know the teachers and their policies. This allowed us all to work together and gave me first-hand experience with things that I could carry through at home. - J.D.

ANSWER: Treat your child as normally as possible. By doing this, other family members will do the same, as well as her peers. Visit with the child's principal, teachers and any specialist who may see her. They can show you and everyone else how to handle the situation. - Richard

Mommy–CEO, adding wisdom: First things first, talk with your child about what's going on. Then after she feels comfortable, you may let her explain it to other family members. In your explanation, be careful not to use names or labels. One of the biggest mistakes made is when parents, teachers, siblings and others label children with learning disabilities with names like stupid, slow, goofy, loser, weirdo and retarded. Why? Because a person with a disability eventually will begin to think of herself as the label we have given her.

Learning disabilities are a challenge that will take a lot of work and acceptance on everyone's part. Stick together and don't label, point fingers or blame, and you will come out just as healthy (and maybe even a little stronger) as a family as before.

QUESTION: Should I exercise during pregnancy?

ANSWER: I enjoy taking long walks outside for my regular exercise routine. In the cooler months, I stay inside on the treadmill. After I found out I was going to have a baby, I tried to stay active but not over do it. Sooner or later I knew I'd probably run out of extra energy. I used to be able to work all day and come home and exercise, but in the later months it was time for me to make a choice. Since I work in an outside sales position, I decided to get my exercise and work done at the same time. This gave me the opportunity to utilize my schedule to incorporate a little extra walking. It worked great. It helped a tremendous amount with my mental state and I never really felt bad or too terribly tired. - B.R.

A professional shares: The question being addressed today is exercise in pregnancy, not dieting in pregnancy. No matter how large you are, dieting is out during pregnancy. Exercise is in (after your doctor's approval). Here's the skinny: Exercise at least three times per week. Use large muscle groups for strengthening your cardiovascular system. Don't overkill. Be able to talk throughout the workout. Limit sessions to 30 minutes. Keep yourself cool with regular sips of water. Safety comes first. Good footwear for exercising along with sure footing are musts! Warm up first and DON'T overextend joints during pregnancy. Keep supine (lying on the floor with your face up) exercises to a minimum after the first trimester. BOND'S TOP THREE exercises during pregnancy are walking, stationary cycling and swimming. Only 15% of women in their 20s and 30s exercise regularly. - Dr. Bond

Mommy–CEO, adding wisdom: It's worth repeating: Check with your doctor to make sure everything is OK and he/she knows what kind of exercise you would like to do. To prevent harming the baby or yourself, the doctor will need to know what type of exercise, if any, you have been doing in the past. Some women feel they need to do more or start "something" right away. If you haven't been too active, walking or a stationary bike might be a good plan for you. I was able to walk throughout my pregnancies.

Note: A recent study suggests that most women should be able to continue exercising during pregnancy or at least through most of it. Please check with your doctor and as long as he/she says it's OK, go for it.

Mommy–CEO for Family Success on Golden Rule Five:

It's the little things that count. Saying "I love you" and giving hugs will be a big plus to family success. Add humor on a daily basis and laugh often with your family team. Spend special time with your children on an individual basis. Listen to what they have to suggest. Give a little time to volunteer opportunities to help make the world a better place. Make time for family fun activities but take a little break for yourself. Build your spirit and soul with words from the Bible  and let God help you to be a stronger parent. Create family traditions and never stop dating your spouse.

DON'T FORGET THE LITTLE THINGS THAT COUNT.

Here are some IMPORTANT DADDY TIPS to share with your hubby:

Dear Husbands,

Please listen to this wise advice and think about what it could mean to your relationship with your beloved wife if you decided to follow it.

1. Help her with the dishes.
2. Tell her she looks really great today.
3. Help give the kids a bath.
4. Volunteer your time in her "volunteer" spot at school.
5. Take care of the baby while she takes a nap.
6. Ask her out on a date.
7. Help clean the house.
8. Help prepare dinner.
9. Take the kids out for a couple of hours by yourself.
10. Tell her often that she is your best friend.
11. Giver her a long kiss with meaning behind it.
12. Bring home fresh flowers at least once a month.
13. Tell her she is your "Everyday Blessing."
14. Give her a back and neck massage.
15. Never leave home without telling her you love her.

These are The Little Things That Count!

A Little Evaluation:

A Child Unaccepted

This is a work based on the ignorance and discrimination the mother of a girl with a rare brain defect faces in the world.

Through her eyes wide with wonder and never ending curiosity she looks. Through eyes filled with tears of a broken heart, I see. Her ears listening to the sounds of the birds singing their springtime songs, the crickets their midnight lullaby, the rustling of the autumn leaves as they settle to the earth and ringing of the sleigh bells in the snow. My ears hear the sound of each teardrop from my eyes falling with a magnified echo into a puddle around me.

She feels the change in the April air as winter turns to spring; she feels the heat of the summer sun warm upon her face. She feels the bite of the autumn air and the icy chill of winter. I feel the change in the air when we enter a crowded room, as the heat is so hot upon my face. I feel the bite of society as we move from one place to another and the icy chill of the unacceptance from many.

She waits impatiently, anticipating the new, wondering what tomorrow will bring. I wait impatiently in dreaded anticipation of what tomorrow will not bring and fight back the tears that flow reflecting upon yesterday. Under a protective wing and a very bold front, together we face the world.

She is taught the goodness of difference and individuality. I am learning the unfortunate truth of being a different individual. She is taught the evil of prejudice, discrimination and ignorance. I am learning hypocrisy. She understands how special a child she is. I know to society, how special she isn't.

Through my eyes wide with wonder and curiosity, and her eyes filled with tears of a broken heart, together we face the world.

© 2001, Suzanne Barata. Used with permission. Suzanne Barata is a mom who is fighting for what is right for her little girl.

Notes

_____

_____

_____

_____

_____

_____

_____

_____

_____

_____

_____

_____

_____

_____

_____

_____

_____

_____

DAILY PRAYER FOR MOMS

The Family, Discipline, and Positive Approaches

It doesn't matter how busy you are,

Don't let the morning get very far.

Take a few minutes to set your tone and pace,

Ask the good Lord to bless your family
with His grace.

He already knows the things that
fill you with despair,

and He's waiting for you to share.

"Dear God, give me the patience needed this day,
to guide and lead me in Your way.

In everything I say and do, please make me
more like you.

Help me with my family challenges
and daily-life grief —

but most of all, please strengthen my belief.
Amen."

FINAL WORDS

I hope you have enjoyed this book and have gained a little more wisdom about parenting and life in general. Life is already a roller coaster of ups and downs, but when we throw in parenting it can really get wacky. Don't forget to reread this book as your children grow and change. For example, if you have teenagers, you may find that some of the most basic points that were taught to them in elementary school need to be implemented again into their schedules. It's true. Teenagers seem to still be developing their brain (this has recently been proven) and often act on impulse and forget guidelines. I work with teenagers, so I know what I'm talking about here. Remember the five golden rules and use them daily at home, work, school and everywhere else with anyone — even your co-workers and spouse. Thank you for purchasing this book and always remember, "Parenting is tough, take the time to listen to your children, don't forget the humor, and never underestimate the power of prayer. Healthy parenting!"

INDEX

Some of My Favorite Web Sites:

www.4kidssites.com — A must-see website for parents, teachers and kids.

www.ABCparenting.com — You'll find lots of good info on sites to go to for anything that you need regarding parenting.

www.amazingmoms.com — Moms are truly amazing, and here you'll find plenty to cheer about.

www.babyuniversity.com — If you have a question about pregnancy or baby, check it out.

www.childrenwithdisabilities.ncjrs.org — You'll find links, advice and events sponsored by government and local organizations.

www.christianitytoday.com — You'll find loads of helpful information and links for almost all of your questions on Christianity, plus links for everyone in the family.

www.crayoncanyon.com — You'll find comic strips about kids and families. Want it in your local newspaper? Ask for it.

www.dotcommommies.com — This is a web site and newsletter that helps you find a work-at-home job.

www.en-parent.com — A site full of info for work-at-home parents.

www.familyvillage.wisc.edu/ — This is a global community of disability resources.

www.fathersworld.com — This is a place for dads and everyone.

www.funfelt.com — A place for parents to order educational and fun, creative boards made of felt with moveable items. Kids love it!

www.funnykids.com — The funny things kids will say and do will make even the most boring situation laughable.

www.giftedchildren.cjb.net/ - Questions and answers for parents of gifted children.

www.icomm.ca/daycare/index.html — This is a thoughtful site for children and caregivers. There are many links and ideas to choose from.

www.kidsource.com — This site is full of information for gifted children.

www.lil-fingers.com — This is a web site for little fingers with animation and fun storybooks.

www.mommameahh.com — Find great, gently used clothes in awesome condition at fair prices.

www.momsonline.com — This is one of the best sites for moms to get quick answers on almost any parenting topic. There is a place for everyone: single, divorced, married, widowed, Christian, professional, etc.

www.mymiraclebaby.com — A unique online shop for babies and tots

www.parenthoodweb.com — This site has tons of parenting answers.

www.parenttoparent.com — This is my web site, which is maintained by an awesome web designer, Cheryl Sandberg. If you need a new design for your site, see the information listed here about Cheryl or go to www.sbdwebdesign.com.

www.peggiesplace.com — If you need ideas as a homeschooler or just a little lift for the day, go look here for faith, fun and fellowship.

www.singleparents.net/index.html — This site offers a place to hang your hat and get information.

www.studyweb.com — This is a site that has tons of answers to homework to benefit the kids and you.

ABOUT THE ILLUSTRATOR

Joyce Abramson recently began her sketching
at the request of a friend. She is an avid
photographer who sings and hums along as she
works. Occasionally, she writes poetry to accompany
her work. Her two children are grown and her
husband's work hours allow her the time to
explore the marvelous world of fine arts.

"Mommy–CEO" (Constantly Evaluating Others) is currently becoming a registered trademark with the United States Patent and Trademark Office in Washington D.C. Keep a watchful eye out on "Mommy–CEO" to be made available on T-shirts, stationary, pens, pencils, mugs, etc.

Look for new book titles by Jodie Lynn coming your way soon. I hope you have enjoyed this book and somehow have gained a little more wisdom on parenting. Thank you for purchasing it.

WRITE TO ME

Please send e-mail to Parentingurway@aol.com if you have parenting tips you'd like to share with the world. Perhaps you'd like to ask a question of your own. I would love to hear from you! Its so wondeful to see how parents and caregivers from all over are networking to help each other. Be our guest, enter one of our contests, and get your story or article published on our web site! See www.parenttoparent.com for details.

ORDERING INFORMATION

The revised edition of *Mommy–CEO (Constantly Evaluating Others)* would make an awesome gift for someone you really care about!

It can be ordered from any bookstore in the United States or Canada or online from amazon.com or barnesandnoble.com.

Visit www.parenttoparent.com for details about quantity discounts for orders of more than 10 copies.